THE JOHN CALVIN MCNAIR LECTURES

SCIENCE AND THE IDEA OF GOD

THE JOHN CALVIN McNAIR LECTURES

Francis H. Smith: *God Manifest in the Material Universe.*

Francis Landey Patton: *Authority and Religion.*

David Starr Jordan: *The Stability of Truth.*

Henry Van Dyke: *The Poetry of Nature.*

Arthur Twining Hadley: *Some Influences in Modern Philosophic Thought.*

Francis G. Peabody: *Christian Life in the Modern World.*

George Edgar Vincent: *The Social Vision.*

John Dewey: *Philosophy and Politics.*

Frederick J. E. Woodbridge: *The Purpose of History.*

Hugh Black: *The Great Questions of Life.*

Edwin Grant Conklin: *The Direction of Human Evolution.*

Paul Shorey: *Plato's Relation to the Religious Problem.*

Charles Allen Dinsmore: *Religious Certitude in an Age of Science.*

Roscoe Pound: *Law and Morals.*

William Louis Poteat: *Can a Man Be a Christian Today?*

Charles Reynolds Brown: *A Working Faith.*

Thornton Whaling: *Science and Religion Today.*

Harris E. Kirk: *Stars, Atoms, and God.*

Robert Andrews Millikan: *Time, Matter, and Values.*

George F. Thomas: *Spirit and Its Freedom.*

Arthur H. Compton: *The Human Meaning of Science.*

William Ernest Hocking: *Science and the Idea of God.*

SCIENCE
AND THE IDEA OF GOD

By

WILLIAM ERNEST HOCKING

CHAPEL HILL
THE UNIVERSITY OF NORTH CAROLINA PRESS
1944

COPYRIGHT, 1944, BY

THE UNIVERSITY OF NORTH CAROLINA PRESS

PRINTED IN THE UNITED STATES OF AMERICA

THE McNAIR LECTURES

THE John Calvin McNair Lectures were founded through
a bequest made by Rev. John Calvin McNair, of the class
of 1849. This bequest became available to the University
in 1906. The extract from the will referring to the foundation is as follows:

"As soon as the interest accruing theron shall by said
Trustees be deemed sufficient they shall employ some able
Scientific Gentleman to deliver before the students then in
attendance at said University, a course of lectures, the
object of which lectures shall be to show the mutual bearing of science and theology upon each other, and to prove
the existence and attributes, as far as may be, of God from
nature. The lectures, which must be performed by a
member of some one of the Evangelic denominations of
Christians, must be published within twelve months after
delivery, either in pamphlet or book form."

PREFACE

In the preface of a book published some years ago under the title, *The Meaning of God in Human Experience,* I suggested that pragmatism as a method of reasoning is half true: negative pragmatism, holding that "what does not work is not true," has a validity which cannot be claimed for the positive maxim that "what works is true."

Of negative pragmatism we have many daily examples. Malaise in one's physical machinery admonishes that one's habits—and the theories which support them—are somewhere wrong: it does not tell one how to set them right. A man who has failed is driven to re-examine his premises; they are in the position of hypotheses not verified, and therefore under suspicion. A man who has succeeded is much inclined to credit his theories as validated by the event, little aware how much those circumstances which constitute his "luck" have spared those theories from effective test. The positive argument is unsafe; the negative argument is safe, for it does not pretend to usurp constructive functions; it merely warns that we must think again.

But if the discovery that our hypothesis is wrong is at the same time a discovery of why it is wrong, negative pragmatism becomes an element in a type of constructive reasoning which philosophers have called "dialectic," the process of self-correction of erroneous ideas in living minds. This process is so useful that it is coming back into general employment after having been frequently read out of court, or even buried, because of the pedantries into which its admirers have been betrayed. The word "dialectic" is quite unnecessary; we might call it a "mental experiment in defective assumptions." But I see no great merit in avoiding it, except the general merit of avoiding technical terms when discussing themes of human import.

In these lectures, we have deliberately entertained an assumption which is plausible, which many believe to be true, which many believe is required by science, that we not only can but must dispense with the traditional belief in God. We might have entitled the book, "Getting on without God." I believe the assumption to be false. But I also believe that Fichte was wrong in supposing that it is a perfectly consistent assumption; that the world can be successfully interpreted on that basis. I believe that trying it out is one of the best ways of seeing that it is not true. That, in brief, is the method of these lectures.

They were originally given as three lectures on the McNair Foundation in Chapel Hill in 1940. In rewriting them, the first lecture grew into two, through examining in greater detail the general attitude of science toward the idea of purpose. In the summer of 1942 they were given before the General Conference of the Congregational Church at Durham, New Hampshire, and at that time a fifth lecture was added, on the subject of immortality.

But while both freedom and immortality constitute subjects for enquiry directly germane to the scientific conscience of our time, those topics must be reserved for future treatment. The present volume is the mature form of the McNair lectures on "Contemporary Science and the Idea of God".

It was Professor G. A. Harrer of the University of North Carolina who first wrote to me in regard to these lectures, and during the Spring of 1943 I was in correspondence with him in regard to their publication. The manuscript had been sent to him. His unfailing courtesy, his hospitality and friendly interest during my residence at Chapel Hill, and his constant kindness during the subsequent period, when the catastrophe of war cut across all plans with its own disturbing imperatives, add to my sorrow that I can no longer place this volume in his hands.

To visit Chapel Hill is to acquire a place of pilgrimage, to which one's thoughts turn with gratitude. And also with warm and enduring affection.

William Ernest Hocking

New York, April 2, 1944.

CONTENTS

SCIENCE AND THE IDEA OF GOD

CHAPTER I

SCIENCE AND RELIGION TODAY: A TRUCE OR A SETTLEMENT?

---

1. *Peace by Appeasement?*

Between science and religion there is today no corporate war. There are still a few scientific hot-heads who would like to put religion into the museum of antiquities: they are no longer representative. Whether there are any corresponding religious hot-heads who would care to suppress science or would conceive it possible to do so I doubt; I have never met one. There are those who gird at "science" in the large, meaning not science at all but an arrogant state of mind sometimes found in scientific men of an earlier vintage: this state of mind will soon be at a premium on account of rarity. No one is today calling for an Either-Or choice between two concerns both of which belong to everybody. We are all scientists by necessity; we are all, after some fashion, religious.

What then has become of that long run of hostilities, the so-called "Conflict between Science and Religion"? Most of it has gone into history, much of it into curious history, though its departing spasm is within our own memories. As a boy, I heard pulpit fulminations against Darwin. My father, whose profession of medicine aligned him with science, yet banned Herbert Spencer from the family bookshelf. The line of debate was not the value of science on its own ground, but the capacity of science to reach a total picture of man and the universe, and to guide human life by that knowledge. This dispute is still with us but is seldom inflamed; it is relieved if not finally closed by a simple jurisdictional agreement. Science withdraws from making assertions about the whole of things, admits that its knowledge does not reach the whole, adding in parentheses a doubt whether "the whole" is a knowable object. Religion (together with philosophy) responds that it is just the whole of things which is—if I may put it that way—its special province, and agrees that it is futile to oppose science on its own ground since science is nothing but organized truth.

The idea of reaching agreement by establishing a separation of provinces is itself so inviting that it assuages tempers even before the boundary is clearly defined. It is hardly satisfactory to say, with a recent author, that "science has decided to stick to its last of building from part to whole, while religion builds from the whole to the part," for this would seem to ensure a collision somewhere in mid-journey. If religion is to have any foothold in human thought, there must be some definable region beyond the scope of science. And on the whole, science today is well disposed to join in an effort to define such a region. Witness the recent conferences on "Science, Philosophy and Religion," valuable if only for the fact of conference itself —remarkable, too, for the general absence of the old polemic bitterness.

Through such conferences it becomes evident that science has no unanimous voice as to what is beyond its own domain, present and future. Certainly it has no official voice. There is, however, a certain convergence of unofficial voices on two such ultra-scientific regions. First, the region commonly assigned to metaphysics, namely, whatever truth can be had either about the whole of things, as just mentioned, or about "the real" as distinct from the phenomenal. Second, the region of "values," that is to say, the estimation of goods and evils, of rights, duties, wrongs, of qualities of pleasure and pain, of beauties and uglinesses, utilities, wastes and detriments—all of these as bearing on a knowledge of the ends worth pursuing, the realm commonly assigned to ethics, aesthetics, and a side of economics. And since values arouse emotion both in anticipation and in enjoyment, this region will include all that side of language and logic which conveys emotion, the language of praise and blame, of epithet, poetry, exhortation, of hope and fear, love and hate, in brief the domain of "emotional meanings" which stands outside the domain of factual meanings proper to science. If ethics and aesthetics founded on purpose and choice are still to be called "sciences," they are of a different order from the sciences of nature founded on causality which have the first right to the name. And religion makes its home in all these aspects of value, offers them a principle of order, declares what goods are most worth having and what are secondary or deceptive, proposes a valid way of life. Religion becomes the *arbiter of ends,* and thus the primary organizer of the practical life of man, an office not less important than that of science itself.

This proposed division of province, I repeat, is not affirmed by any corporate voice of science. I ought to note however that there is one voice crying in our time which has offered its services to science, and would be glad to be taken as official: this voice is "logical positivism." It began a quarter-century ago by denouncing both parts of our beyond-science territory, both totality-statements and value-statements, as "meaningless": the region beyond science is empty. This simple result was reached by an equally simple device: one had only to define "meaning" in such a way that totality-statements and value-statements could not possibly qualify—a political ingenuity introduced into supposedly serious thinking. Nothing was to be admitted as having "meaning" unless it brought you around to verifiable sense-data. The definition palpably begged the question, but many unwary minds were taken in the trap: metaphysics and religion, together with ethics, were neatly dismissed as nonsense, and humanity at a stroke was spared infinite fruitless discussion. Positivism thus made itself heir to the older and lingering anti-religious bias of Continental Europe.

But science has not as yet accepted this voice as its own. It perceives, I suspect, that in both these denials positivism was out of date at its birth. Positivism itself has begun to wake up to the old truth that men must live by their values, and to draw the logical conclusion that if (as it has been saying) value-judgments are meaningless, then human life is meaningless. This is uncomfortable, but there is no way out of it on the assumed premises. Finding itself thus in the awkward position of identifying the valuable with the meaningless and the meaningful with the valueless, positivism today effects a strategic retreat by way of another definition, that of "importance": it allows that something may be "important" without being "scientifically meaningful." Under this clause, even religion is permitted to enter as "possibly important." But was it not about the middle of the nineteenth century when science inclined to describe its attitude toward metaphysics and the like as "agnostic"? And does not this imply that religion is "possibly important"? And is not the present effort to outline a province for religious thought a distinct stage ahead? As a leader of opinion, positivism slowly catches up with the led.

In point of fact, science is today concerned to see this task through. It not only admits, but insists, that science is not a complete guide to human living. This mood of humility is not unmingled with prudence; feeling the peril of our time, scientists also perceive the peril to science itself of being widely relied on for a sort of guidance it cannot give. Its proper business is to show the connections of events, so that men can use events as means to their ends. What these ends may be science does not specify; if it has ever led men to suppose that it can teach them what objects are worth pursuing, it is now eager to disavow any such capacity.

For its part, religion is equally careful to move out of any field that might bring it into conflict with science. It has become wary of making capital of the momentary dilemmas of science, or of staking out claims in science's unfinished work. Formerly religion was inclined to consider that every domain taken over by science as a field for impersonal causal law was so much territory subtracted from the scope of divine control. It therefore fought a loyal campaign of retreat, and made the most of any unexplained residues of Nature: the sources of life could not be explained; the mysterious origins of species; the marvelous fitness of the world for living beings; the emergence of human reason. Religion now realizes that it cannot live in temporary quarters from which it may be driven by the next scientific advance; nor can it subsist on the left-overs of uncompleted laboratory business.

This policy makes it hesitant in its claim to deal factually with "the whole of things," if this can be considered the ultimate goal of scientific description. Such a claim would seem to invite a conflict with science even if only at the Last Day! In some sense religion is obliged to deal with the whole; for anxiety about the whole in which he is placed is precisely what makes the human animal human, distinguishes him from the brute. The answer may be that religion is to deal with the whole as a realm of value rather than of fact. Such an understanding leaves it undisputed master in the field of ends, and sets it free to welcome the growing penetration of science into the problems of life, mind, and reason.

At the risk of troubling waters that are becoming serene, I fear I must denounce this division of labor. Peace on these terms has the character of a truce, not of a settlement. It means that in subscribing to the doctrine that "science is truth," which is correct, religion has also agreed that "truth

is science," which is an overstatement: it means that religion has no truth of its own, a position which is intolerable.

Much contemporary religion bears the moral mark of
an illegitimate surrender. It has abandoned at the behest
of science first immortality, since for science there is no
other world than this world, and mind and body are inseparable; then freedom, since science under the name of
psychology takes over all of human nature into the natural system of causes and effects; and finally God as anything more than a name for our highest values. It was at
first inclined to hand these three notions over to metaphysics; it has ended by abandoning metaphysics itself as
a house built too near the crater of Vesuvius.

For a century and a half since Kant, first ethical then
psychological and sociological interpretations of religion
have been pressed to provide substitutes for the doctrinal
elements of faith. Religious ideas become "postulates,"
that is to say, demands made on the world, launches of
will, wills to believe. Or religion itself is a phenomenon
of self-consciousness, a factor of social adjustment, a semi-
beneficent illusion: we cannot say, "There is a God," but
we can say, "Man is a praying animal"; scare him enough
and he prays, revealing something "deep in subconscious-
ness" and therefore highly authentic. Of such anthropo-
logical verity is much contemporary religious thought constructed, science now holding the whip of a resigned authority. Religion shows gratification when the anchor of
its drifting boat catches in a submerged tree!

Shall we be satisfied with this situation? To my mind

this is less than peace by appeasement; it is peace by capitulation. So far as religion follows these paths, it yields that without which it cannot survive, and strengthens the current swing to a new dogmatism which confesses a desire to seem strong without being strong. Nothing can be won by falling back on Maginot Lines of Barthian pseudofinality. In recognizing the capitulation, we gain nothing by forgetting that it is incidental to an advance. Religion is enriched by the abundance of relevant data, and new relationships brought to light by sceintific enquiry. There can be no question of going back on what science has shown, nor on what it has contributed to religion. The question is solely, what is it that science has shown, and what is the truth which lies beyond that boundary?

I propose to examine the idea of God in the light of several sciences and their applications. But it will help our enquiry if we first note how the present situation arose.

2. *The Dialectical Experiment*

There are several ways to enquire whether the name "God" stands for any real being. One is to appeal to reason, whether by analyzing the nature of the world or by attempting a proof of God's existence. Another way is by a positive appeal to experience, to discover whether we have or may have any immediate awareness of God. In an age which gives the highest rating to empirical evidence, this way has its recommendations; it has however a disadvantage in communicating conviction from one person to another; experiences of God cannot be pointed out and shared like experiences of physical objects. But the appeal to experience may also be made in a negative fashion: *try to get along without God and see what happens.* This is the method of dialectical experiment. "Dialectic" is a rather pedantic term for a natural procedure: ride your hypothesis until it shows its fallacy—if it does, then correct it. The assumption is that a false hypothesis will sooner or later run into a dead end or reverse itself. This may prove to be a long and expensive way of discovering a mistake—experience has never been a cheap teacher: its great advantage is that when one can neither prove or disprove by a positive syllogism or a *reductio ad absurdum,* it promises convincing results if one is sufficiently persistent.[1] We propose in these lectures to follow the method of dialectical experiment. But in our case, the experiment of getting on without God has been by now fairly well tried out in several directions in our modern world, so that we have chiefly to garner the results of the experiences of others.

Since the seventeenth century, natural science has been carrying on this experiment within its own field. It has deliberately undertaken to get along without God: it has rejected anything resembling mind or purpose as a factor in physical happenings. The early campaigners, Galileo, Descartes, Bacon, Spinoza, were hot to drive all purposive elements, the "final causes" of Aristotle's world-view, out of the list of hypotheses which science could properly con-

1. What is called "dialectic" in the schools is frequently a résumé of the results of some other person's costly experience: Socrates, who was skilled in the method, knew how to lead his respondent swiftly from his false premise to its unacceptable consequence, and thus to abbreviate the pain of prolonged floundering which actual experience might require.

sider. They insisted on looking at natural events causally, and leaving this causal contemplation mathematically clear. The world of change is a world of strict law: it moves from what is given to what is due to follow with the minutest precision, and without the slightest concern whether that following event is better or worse.

To be sure, they overdid their necessities. They could not prove that purposes are absent from nature. They could only show that as scientific hypotheses purposes were superfluous and beclouding. The planetary motions were better understood by Kepler's geometry alone than by mixing with it his notions of attendant spirits: Kepler himself in the end dismissed his romance of intelligent guidance for these motions. No one of the great innovators from Copernicus to Newton was disposed to exclude God from the universe, but only to clear Nature from his interference. But the argument was none the less extrusive in effect: for who can believe in a purpose, or a Purposer, which science can neglect not alone with impunity but with advantage? This experiment of getting along without God worked remarkably well: it released the springs of modern science.

This emphatic dismissal of God as a factor in events was brought to a clear formula by that clearest-headed analyst of problems, Immanuel Kant. All the old proofs of God were based, he showed, on some *relation* which God was supposed to sustain to events or to the whole world of events. God was taken to be the "cause" of the world, or the "designer" of the world—in each case related to the world in an intelligible and significant way.

But this, Kant declared, is just the trouble with the proofs: all the intelligible relationships, such as "before and after," "cause and effect," "means and end," belong within the world, not between the world and an outside being. Whatever stands in any such understandable relation to specific events or things falls within the system we refer to as "Nature," and so comes under the survey of science. And since these relations connect part to part, or event to event, *within* Nature, it is a misuse of terms to apply them to Nature-as-a-whole and some unimaginable outside being: there are causes of events, but no causes of causation! This leaves it that, if God exists, he can stand in *no intelligible relation* either to specific events, or to the world as a whole. Proofs of God's existence based on such supposed relationships will therefore be invalid.

Now Kant was a student of science, an avid reader of Newton, and a careful analyst of scientific procedure. He knew that when the physicist spoke of a world of "law," he had in mind the ideal perfection with which causal relations lend themselves to mathematical expression. If causality is, as it seems to be, a self-operating flow, in which God is not at all involved, Kant's discussion shows us, in a brilliantly convincing manner, *why* the scientific experiment of getting along without God was so successful within its own limits. The question whether there are still other fields of experience in which such an experiment ought to be tried is left open. Kant, as we know, was of the opinion that in ethical experience the attempt would be a flat failure. He himself had no intention of giving up the idea of God, nor had Spinoza or Leibniz or Newton. But he made it very difficult for himself, and for all others who held both to science and to God, to say what a God could mean who is not intelligibly related to the world of Nature or the events within it. A God who could be ignored in the planning of life would seem to come as near as possible to being no God at all. We must give Kant the credit of having first raised the prior question whether the belief in God is not literally meaningless.

He was certainly not the first to feel the difficulty, nor the first to try resolving it by *altering his idea of God.* If God does not intrude in the course of Nature, he is not that Special Providence we have thought him; he is not a momentary responder to momentary prayer. But we may think of him in other ways. Spinoza went so far as to say that if we have the right idea of God his reality will become at once obvious—another way of stating the famous "ontological argument"; or to put the matter obversely, so long as you doubt the existence of God you may be sure you have not the right idea of God. For Spinoza, God is not a being outside of the world and therefore related to it in some way as events are related to each other: God is the true being, the very substance of the world itself, the inner nature of Nature. To believe in Nature is to believe in God. Spinoza's God escapes in advance all of Kant's strictures.

This expedient of redefining the idea of God has become a fairly general one in our day, for we have become peculiarly word-conscious and definition-conscious. The question, Do you believe in God? will seldom get a direct answer from a thoughtful contemporary without the preliminary counter-question, What do you mean by God? And many a man, including many a scientist, together with Professor Dewey and Professor Alexander, is ready to use the word God or Deity if you allow him to define it in his own way.

This is a substantial advance in the whole outlook; a new elasticity is brought into discussions which had become deadlocked and fruitless. At the same time, a word of caution is necessary, since the liberty of definition of the idea of God cannot be unlimited. If, for example, God is defined as "the order of the universe," anyone who believes that the universe has some kind of order forthwith becomes a believer in God—certainly too easily. Or if, with Spinoza, we identify God and Nature, we can hardly be sure without further examining Spinoza's view of Nature that we still have a God—a problem which baffled Spinoza's contemporaries. If Nature is an order of purely causal necessity—and some read Spinoza that way—then surely we have no God; for the term God implies a concern for the moral relations among events, an element of justice in the long-time strands of conscious history, in brief a *moral order* as well as a causal order. If God is the causal order of Nature, then every scientist postulates God at the beginning of his labor. If God is the moral order of the world, the consent of the scientist is not automatic, since moral connections do not come within his ken as a scientist.

Consider the well-known confession of faith of Einstein: "I believe in God, the God of Spinoza, who reveals himself in the orderly harmony of the Universe. . . . I believe that intelligence is manifested throughout all nature. . . . The basis of all scientific work is the conviction that the world is an ordered and comprehensible entity, and not a thing of chance." Here Einstein, while invoking science and Spinoza, appears to go beyond both. For while it belongs to science (and Spinoza) to assume that the things and events within the world have orderly and comprehensible connections, and that no such thing or event is a matter of chance, it belongs to neither science nor Spinoza to judge that the world as a whole is placed in a *comprehensible* order, or that its existence is an actual manifestation of intelligence. When the phrase, "not a thing of chance," is taken with the other phrase, "intelligence is manifested," the combined suggestion is one of intelligent choice, not of impersonal necessity; and intelligent choice implies purpose or consciousness of value. If Einstein means that the existence of the world manifests purpose, and not merely that the succession of events manifests an intelligible order, he comes nearer the usual conception of God than does Spinoza.

Modern Buddhism has sometimes tried to recommend itself to the scientifically minded by pointing out that its view of the universe is one of law, that it denies the personal God professed by most religions, but asserts that the universe *does* impersonally (and therefore justly) what the personal gods were supposed to do on sporadic volition. It teaches that there are unchangeable principles such as Karma and the Four-fold Truth upon which the human being can absolutely rely. This is law, and the view is on the whole a view well-reasoned; but here its affiliation with science comes to an end. The whole genius of the "laws of Nature" as science finds them is that they are indifferent to the ethical quality of what they regulate, whereas the law proclaimed by Buddhism is, after all, a moral law. Karma must take cognizance of the moral quality of deeds and motives, as no purely causal law can do; I fear we must say flatly that no unconscious or impersonal agency could make the necessary discriminations. Just in so far as Buddhism is a religion, it departs from what a purely scientific world-view would prescribe.

And this is substantially our present situation: religion and science cannot reach the accord for which both are prepared by simply equating God with Nature, or with that marvelous but traceable order discerned in the system of the natural world. If we can get along without God in the work of scientific hypotheses, we can equally well get along without him as thus redefined.

3. *What is God more than Nature?*

Religion, we say, cannot be content with an idea of God which is simply a selective way of emphasizing the orderliness of the natural world. In point of fact, those who make such a proposal, scientists or philosophers, never do so, I believe, on a purely factual basis: they do so on the basis of an emotion which Nature stirs in them, an emotional response toward infinitude and mystery, which is extrascientific, though it lies at the root of many a scientist's choice of vocation. The physical universe is capable of evoking—not when we grasp it least, but when we grasp it most adequately—a response of almost personal devotion toward its majesty, its vastness, its beauty, its marvelous perfection, its unfathomed depths of intricate harmony, its stupendous rhythms and moving equilibria. This cosmic emotion is indeed religious and no religion is complete without it. But emotion is prophetic of thought; it is incipient idea; and this emotion forecasts further elements in the idea of God which must enter into our definition.

God has something to do with the *meaning* of things. Physical science has nothing to do with meaning or value as distinct from fact. If the object of physical science excites emotion, this is a sign that meaning is there, somehow, as if in defiance of our resolve to be rigidly factual. But *how* is it there if we are to use the term God?

Psychology may offer a suggestion. Psychology is a science, and it encounters the fact of meaning. It deals with human beings, and finds them showing desire and aversion. These responses are facts, a curious kind of fact which has the property of polarizing the objects of the physical world, endowing them with qualities desirable and undesirable. To the desiring creature, nothing appears neutral; there are no "mere facts." To the creature of instinct and passion, all facts are surcharged with relevance to his loves and hates; the world is alive with "meaning." But this fact does not, to the psychologist nor to us, call for the use of the term God. It is true, no psychologist can say why desire exists—a perfect automaton could work as well with no consciousness at all; but given desire, then the values and meanings of experienced objects are precisely what they have to be; they become a part of the necessary order of natural events.

But if this is the final account of meaning, not only is there no need for religion, but also no need for meaning itself. Once we adopt the psychological account as complete, we begin to distrust the whole structure of our values. They depend on the accident of our constitution; they have no validity of their own. Seen in this light, the values themselves appear to topple and lose their command. It is as though we could pursue with full zest only those objects whose value is "real," in the sense of not depending on ourselves alone. It is this which first justifies invoking the idea of God, if the presence of God in the world could confer a certain stability upon the contrasts of good and bad, right and wrong, noble and base. Suppose we should think of God as the *element of objectivity* in the order of values. Then the psychological facts may be as they are. But we see that "Nature," thus enlarged, carries within it a standard of validity for our appreciations, and the cosmic emotion we were speaking of appears justified in its object. Without God, meaning is simply a human specialty, the vast universe is devoid of meaning. With God, the world has sense, perhaps a direction. And the wide frame of meaning returns upon our small lives to lend them significance; for meaning descends from the whole to the parts.

For psychology, meaning hails from another quarter— from sensation. What does the whistle "mean"? Time to quit work and eat. What does the whip "mean"? The pain of the lash. That is "good" which leads to pleasurable sense-experience, and vice versa. Come on a pleasure or a pain and you strike something substantial in the field of value, just as when you strike a "sense-datum," you come on something substantial in the field of knowledge: the sense-stuff is what the ideas mean, point to, terminate in. We need no God to inform us of the value of beefsteak to the hungry: here is a tangible unit with which science can operate. Good: I agree to this. An existence without sense-qualia would be empty, indefinite, colorless. But how substantial is this unit? Is it pertinent to ask, in turn, *What do your sensations "mean"?* Does any sense-pleasure, shining by its own light, continue to shine as it is indefinitely repeated? Does the value of activity lie in the confused mixture of sensation that goes with it, pain of effort, joy of motion, or rather does it lie in the awareness of power to work toward objects gainable, which objects themselves fit into a plan? Does the plan mean a group of sense-data, or do the sense-data mean the plan? In all meaning, sense and idea coöperate, but none can escape the last dependence on the significance of the whole. Whatever else, then, we put into the idea of God, we cannot omit his role as sustaining the total scheme of our values.

Perhaps the notion of God should be confined to this function, which wholly escapes conflict with the concerns of science. This is the modern version of Plato's conception of God, the ideal Good (including the True and the Beautiful) in its eternal essence, the changeless object of all desire, the goal of all striving. And to this Aristotle adds the trait of the "unmoved mover," the pure Form toward which all things tend by the universal urge to perfection. God, then, is no power among powers; he does not himself compete; he acts only—as Lao Tze said—by non-assertion, by the inherent attraction of his own being, the silent but inescapable persuasion of the Good. God is the absolute argument for rightness, embedded in the nature of the living universe.

4. *The Dilemma for the Modern Mind*

Such a conception of God does indeed seem to have a substantial content; but it is at the cost of excluding God from any action in the realm of fact. This seems to many minds a moral as well as scientific advantage: God is not power, he does not compete with the earthquake and the fire; his is the still, small voice. The notion of power, it is argued, disfigures the divine ideal.

And yet, to surrender God's power of action seems to surrender the whole realm of nature and history to the undivine forces which contend there. Is God to be powerless because power in finite control may be a source of horror? Surely, if we consider the history of religion, the argument runs in the reverse sense: just *because* Nature's power is insensate, while the power of historic agencies is frequently cruel and always ignorant, a divine power is requisite which can overrule catastrophe and mischief. Indeed, unless there is some assurance in the factual nature of things that the good can be achieved and built into the facts, the very attraction of the ideal begins to appear a delusive lure, and God as the persuasion to good becomes a guide to tragedy.

If we accept this argument, and I confess that to me it is conclusive, the Platonic God can no longer satisfy us. On the other hand, to allow in God an element of control of fortune or of operation in the course of events would seem to take us back to the realm of miracle and so revive the clash with science. This is the dilemma for the modern mind in the idea of God.

It may be formulated as a set of opposing demands which the man of today must make, on account of his allegiance on the one hand to science and on the other, to the realm of meanings:

(1) *God must not intrude* in the causal sequences which concern the natural sciences. Neither the observer in the laboratory nor the maker of hypotheses must be called on to refer any effect to his activity.

(2) *God must act.* It is a persuasion of our time amounting to a fundamental insight that whatever is real is active: if God were not active, we could not think him real.

The recognition of this predicament is seen in the seriousness with which religion is taken today, especially by its enemies. They are *no longer tolerant of it as a mental luxury*. It could once be passed off as an aspiring and reverent sentiment which did a man no harm, and might do some good: we now see that there are no harmless sentiments. If belief in God is not truth it is an evil. Our age is prepared to specify certain definite *harms which religion, if not true, must inflict on the race*. Its indictment runs as follows:

Religion cultivates indirect ways of thinking. Instead of asking directly what is good and relying on his own judgment of value, the believer must ask, "What is the will of God?" and seek in the dark for an answer—a futile gesture of deference to an unknowable absolute judge.

Religion accents the amiable attitudes in a world which

requires conflict. Religion gives no guide to the struggle which must be waged if good is to be realized in a world such as this. The professionally religious become characterized by a certain softness and timorous disloyalty through specializing in the emotions of agreement, indiscriminately exercised toward just and unjust. It obscures the truth that morality can win its spine only in the school of opposition accepted and met in kind.

It encourages neglect of self-help, including the wholehearted pursuit of science as the chief resource for overcoming the evils which afflict the race. For "try," it reads "pray for help"; for "think," "pray for guidance."

It continues to hope for another world, in spite of the fact that it says less about it than formerly. This lurking spirit of other-worldliness runs through the religious veins like a sedative, diminishing the sense of the uniqueness of the present opportunity of life, and the insistence of the present problems. The "opiate" is still there; and Rousseau is still justified in judging that he wanted no Christians in his ideal state, for their real citizenship was elsewhere.

These criticisms are serious enough to stir any sincere mind out of holding to a belief in God purely on inertia. They have in fact led to two types of change. Some have held to the demand that God acts, but acts in a different sphere than the sphere of science. Some have undertaken to carry on in personal life the scientific experiment of getting along without God. If this tentative atheism is mistaken, the course of experience should show the nature of the mistake. This would be the dialectical way to recover the truth. Let us look at both of these efforts.

5. *Efforts to Escape the Dilemma*

One way of meeting the dilemma, we have said, is to change one's conception of God's sphere of activity. The almost universal primitive assumption is that overt benefits are God's special province—help in livelihood, love, and war, the birth of sons, protection in all hazards—without boggling over the methods by which God is to accomplish these ends. Disillusionment on this score is one factor—not the only factor—in altering the direction of prayer. God is not to be the valet for my private wishes; he is not to disrupt for human ends the order of Nature established by him from the foundation of the world. All thoughtful religious consciousness is inclined to consider God's action in a less physical form than primitive notions assume, even while maintaining with Xenophon's Socrates that "the gods have reserved for themselves the most important events," so that all eventualities before which man's power and wisdom fail are proper objects of prayer. With a still more mature religious sense God's sphere is defined as that of the spirit. I may pray to him for spiritual benefits, for renewal of faith, for strength against temptation, for the regeneration of my heart, perhaps for mental power (cathedrals in Europe show tablets of thanks left by students at certain shrines for *succes d'examen*).

Thus the "inner life" becomes the peculiar field of divine effect. And as the questions of science have been pressed in our Western world, there was a time within living memory when this seemed a secure retreat; for what God did "in the heart" was no concern of science. God could "inspire" and "reveal"; God could give "grace" so that one was able to forgive and to love his neighbor; God could discover to the mind ways to meet difficulties insuperable to human wisdom; above all, God could convert and save.

But this retreat inward seemed to preserve the requirements of science only because the science of psychology was left out of the reckoning. If psychology is to bring the causal type of lawfulness into the workings of the mind, then as psychology moves into the field of religious experience, the mystics must move out.

This eviction is not the first word of psychology to religion. It began its services by promising to rescue religion from the speculative and dubious services of metaphysics, and to give it a firm grounding in the self-validating experience of man. It explains away the exuberance of imagery in myth and doctrine; but it translates these mythical meanings into terms of hope and despair, of ethical struggle and triumph, and so covers the retreat of faith from the unstable world of supernature to the safe refuge of inner certitude. God becomes a name for a verifiable influence welling up from the subconscious life, bringing about peace, exaltation, and renewal.

But in the course of performing these very real services, it could not be long before the question was raised *why the old religious imagery should be retained* as a poetic nomenclature for phenomena which are capable of exact description. The advent first of psychotherapy and then of psychoanalysis completed this phase of advance. The conceptual apparatus of the creeds has been dropped and the cure of souls established upon a wholly scientific basis.

Thus the first way of meeting the dilemma of the two postulates passed into the second way, the experiment of getting on without God. The question which we propose to trace is whether this type of experiment is successful. Or whether, if it is not successful, it leads as by a dialectical necessity to a sounder conception of the nature of God's action in the world. We begin by examining the psychological experiment.

CHAPTER II

PSYCHOLOGY AND THE
CURE OF SOULS

---

1. *Psychology for Prediction and Control*

Psychology is the characteristic science of our time. Man first looks outward and makes a science of the inanimate objects around him; his first great successes, in modern times, are in astronomy and physics. For a time the mysteries of biology and physiology, with their close relation to the art of medicine, hold themselves apart from physics, and chemistry is slow in taking scientific shape. Nature appears to have built quality into the chemical ingredients of the world, like a palette of many colors; and life refuses to reduce itself into simple motions, collisions, attractions and repulsions. But by degrees these sciences also are drawn into a series with physics. At last, man turns the methods of external science upon himself, his mental self: psychology is born.

Human self-knowledge did not, of course, begin with the modern science of psychology. Casual observations about behavior and character are as old as the race; folklore is a magazine of unsystematic notes on human nature. What is modern is the assumption that states of mind are "phenomena" in cause-and-effect relations with other phenomena, mental or physical, and subject to exact measurement. The new science is lured on by an ideal, that of a physics of the emotions, thoughts, impulses.

In this new guise as a natural science, psychology has its peculiarities. The progress of physics depends on the circumstance that its observations and measurements can be verified by other observers and measurers. But in psychology, the business of observing the mind is awkward to begin with, and measurement as applied to mental states and energies has its still refractory puzzles. The object of observation, if it is one's own mind, cannot be directly perceived by anyone else: what I say about my own states cannot be verified by any other observer—neither can it be denied. For exact science, this is a handicap. It might be considered a compensation that psychology is the only science in which the object to be observed, oneself, is completely open to inspection, without apparatus, to at least one observer. Yet the modern science suspects this advantage, is inclined to disparage or even to deny it; resorts to those same indirect methods of hypothesis and verification which have surprised so many secrets of external nature, as if for the mind also the important truths are well-hidden by nature, and have to be pried out by skillful guessing. The "subconscious" admirably supplies the need for a concealed inner core, within whose obscurities there is the same chance for startling discovery as within the subatomic world: one sometimes suspects that if there were no subconscious (as Voltaire said of God) psychology would be obliged to invent one, if only to keep its methods in line with those of physics.

And is the motive for learning these secrets the same in the case of the self as in the case of physical nature? The motives of physics are first of all the discovery of truth, then prediction, and finally control of events by the application of discovered law. Does psychology also propose not alone to know, but also to predict and to control? The answer seems to be "Yes" in each case.

As for prediction, wherever there is law there is prediction; for a causal law is by its own nature a general statement of the form, "If X occurs, Y will follow." If there are laws of this sort in psychology, there will be prediction, always of course with the proviso, "other things being equal," a proviso that may play a more important role in the complexities of mental nature than elsewhere. For example, "If a dog has been conditioned by hearing the sound of a bell whenever he is offered food, then if the bell sounds alone, salivation will follow." Or "Given a sudden, loud noise, startle will follow" (provided the subject is not warned in advance). Or, "A robust voice is essential to the prestige of an officer; a weak voice commands no respect" (unless the officer has enough character to make up for it). Or, "Bombing a civilian population from the air will intimidate them, and bring about speedy surrender" (unless it has the opposite effect of stirring them to more determined resistance). The provisos do seem at times to nullify the value of the prediction; but this does not destroy the predictive nature of law, if law there is in mental events.

As for the motive of *control,* psychology today has applications in abundance. It is true, no science can be held responsible for the uses men try to make of its results.

But current and accepted applications are a part of what scientific enquiry means to its own age; and every application (as a deduction from the body of hypotheses constituting the science) is an incidental test—perhaps a verification—of the hypothesis employed. Psychology is accordingly not disinclined to recommend its own enquiries by their utility in the guidance of human life. In education it has become an indispensable source of advice for the practice of teaching, if not for its aims and standards. In industrial processes, its work has gone far. In social and ethical guidance it has not as yet undertaken so much, but it looks forward with full confidence here also to supplanting our cruder techniques. As Professor Leuba has somewhere said:

The systematic introduction of scientific management for the establishment of accepted individual and social ideals in the mind of the young, for purging the individual from evil tendencies, and for the organization of the life-impulses into harmonious personalities, will mark a new era in the history of humanity in comparison with which the industrial revolution will seem of little significance.

It is especially in the sphere of the cure of souls that psychology through its applications in psychiatry, psychotherapy and psychoanalysis, has recently shown a large capacity to help. And as the cure of souls may fairly be regarded as the precise sphere of practical religion, we are especially concerned with it. There is this difference, that religion enlarges the scope of the soul's suffering. It declares the soul most in need of healing when it is most satisfied with itself, and is likely to regard the beginning of anxiety as the first stage toward recovery from mortal danger. The psychiatrist recognizes disease only where there is a conscious malaise and awareness of maladjustment or inner conflict, and feels it at least a symptom of recovery when his patient is once more at ease with the world. But for both, there are special conditions of unhappiness or despair which call for remedy, and here psychiatrist and priest meet on the same ground.

In these acute phases of psychosis, mental and physical disorder are both present. An unnerving fear of the world or of the future or of God's wrath is no doubt a mental state, induced by ideas; but it cannot exist without physical disturbance, as effect and perhaps also as part-cause. Social incapacities, feelings of inferiority, obsessions by resentment or hatred, delusions of persecution, are sure to show accompanying physiological abnormalities, and may bring about chronic physical ailment. The wide scope of these physical consequences is only beginning to be known. Making the distinction between organic disease and functional disease, it has been recently said that "more than half the disease the medical profession is called on to deal with is functional in origin." Now functional diseases are chiefly due to maladjustments of one kind or another between the individual and the circumstances of his life, a matter which as a rule is beyond the reach of the physician: the sources of all such illness and its organic consequences thus elude medical control. And though many a physician feels driven to become psychologist and sociologist to deal with such troubles, he is more inclined to refer the matter to the psychiatrist, in the hope that revision of the patient's attitude may heal both mind and body at once.

There was a time when the physician would have been

likely to call in the priest, and indeed he still does so occasionally. And conversely, the wise priest often found himself in the role of a physician, just because he was necessarily something of a psychologist. But, as Jung has found in a community fairly typical, the non-Catholic population is more likely, in mental suffering, to consult the psychiatrist than the representative of religion. There is a wide persuasion that this application of psychology has made good its claim to replace the empirical methods of traditional "spiritual" advice with methods scientifically guided and therefore more successful. Let us consider the advantages which are claimed.

2. *Advantages claimed for Psychiatry*

Perhaps the greatest of these advantages is the *objectivity* of the scientific approach to the patient. Treated as an invalid rather than as a sinner, he is relieved at once of the shame which impedes self-revelation. This may be half the battle, for the sense of guilt leads to concealment, concealment to worry, and worry to abnormality. No doubt the patient has in some sense gone wrong, and he has done so through some aberration of desire. But desire (it is said) is an inexpugnable fact of human nature, and what directions it makes for itself is a matter for advisement, not for condemnation. Approached by an enquirer rather than by a judge, the avowal of data ceases to be a "confession." The patient may join the physician in the search for the relevant facts; what one has been concealing from others may have become hidden from oneself, and if such treasures are uncovered the strains of repression are at once relieved.

A second advantage is the *rationality* of the treatment, the fitting of means to ends. The religious officer has not been in the habit of examining the causes of going wrong, nor the removal of those causes as the essence of his cure. He has rather been concerned with the quality of wrongness itself, the displeasure of God which it entails, and the necessity of intercession for forgiveness, together with the appropriate remorse and rejection of the moral evil. On the whole, those who find themselves in the wrong prefer to dwell on the causes for their departure rather than on its culpability; for a cause is in some sense an excuse. The cause-and-effect method of treatment has thus a double recommendation.

A third advantage is in the *mercy* of the cure. The change that is required of him involves no wholesale renunciation of an old will: it is a relatively simple and natural reinterpretation of his desires. The element of discontinuity with his previous self is minimized: it is not "conversion" by supernatural agency that is expected, nor even repentance and absolution, but rather a form of self-conserving under such names as "sublimation," "socialization," "integration." Sublimation consists in conserving the energies of those impulses which have gone astray, instead of uprooting them. Socialization likewise preserves these impulses and gives them a social rather than a solitary mode of satisfaction. This way of reading the outcome is directly in line with the patient's own direction, since the willingness to see a physician already implies that he is beginning to see the need of turning to the social world for the cure of his private state.

Thus, the theological excess is dissolved, and the scientific equivalent is presented as it were with the benefit of anesthesia—a method freed from shame, from fear, and from remorse, indeed from every vestige of the pain of moral self-judgment. The imagery of religion, compelling one to grope for tangible meanings, is replaced by the experiential terminology of science. One understands what the term "God" stood for, in terms of "projections" and "regressions"; and joy in salvation is made clear in terms of "hallucinatory fulfilment." To some minds, at least, this constitutes an advance in intelligibility.

Allowing for the sake of the argument that this procedure does constitute a simplification and rationalization of the traditional procedures of religion, let us examine somewhat more closely the instruments by which the psychiatrical cures are effected.

3. *Fundamental Procedures of Psychoanalysis*

With a somewhat violent summarization which forces into a generic picture the methods of highly divergent schools, we may for our purposes recognize three usual steps of procedure, self-analysis, explanation, re-education.

Self-analysis replaces confession, and purports to be a radical advance upon it. In the confessional the penitent tells what he knows: in the clinic the patient is led to reveal what he does not know. In either case, the patient is the sole source of information about himself. But the whole program of analysis depends on an assumption which the religious tradition has but vaguely appreciated, that the most pertinent details may be buried under mental refuse or kept in locked chests whose key is lost. The psycho-analytic art consists of devices for recovering these clues, devices which have become common knowledge, in essence a set of prolonged, laborious efforts for resuscitating the encysted self. The guarded and guarding self is set to work in a guarded way to lure the off-guard self into evidence. Hence dreams and the telling of dreams, hypnosis, semi-hypnosis, carefully cultivated idle musings, artfully in-duced naïvetés; and then, quite essential, a resolute and terrible candor in reporting what floating thoughts and images are there. In such a procedure, mental flotsam be-comes the treasure trove.

From these data, the psychiatrist—whose special code of translation gives meaning to the apparent rubbish—now reconstructs the secret springs of the ailing personality. The essential point is that with the priest the penitent re-mains at the level of rational conversation. With the psy-choanalyst the patient is induced to speak in symbols whose interpretation is unknown to him, and on this basis he is asked to accept a version of his motive self which he may with difficulty recognize. It is necessary to the work of the priest that the penitent retain his conscious moral identity: "It is I who have done this thing." It is necessary to the work of the analyst that the patient dip into discontinuity, and recover himself on the other side of a blank as it were a partial stranger: "Is this indeed I whom I see in the ana-lytic mirror?" Otherwise, why be analyzed?

The second step is that of "explanation." Explanation brings the patient to the position of the analyst in his con-ception of the sickness. Taking a scientific view of himself, he sees his error as a case of misjudgment which has its causes and is therefore to be contemplated with a degree of toleration. He gains the benefit of classification; his problem is a common human problem, and his previous solution, though erroneous, a common mistake. He is reminded that all human nature has its heights and depths, with perhaps an additional comment to the effect that "there can be no heights without depths," in which case, clearly, a depth is almost a necessity. He begins to feel of himself as of others that to know all is to forgive all, or rather, to transcend the need of forgiveness, since the discovery of the causes has displaced the category of wrong.

The essential element here is the achievement of objective categories of description, i.e., changing one's categories from the moral to the factual. It has been described as the attainment of "a normally disillusioned life." It might be called the attitude of Spinoza directed to oneself, seeing oneself "under the aspect of eternity" as a series of events springing from the eternal necessity, and thus to be considered without aversion and without remorse.

The patient is now ready for the beginning of the positive curative process, the step of re-education. In understanding himself, he has been relieved of the superfluous pains of self-condemnation, but this does not imply full satisfaction with the past. The motives which led him to consult his physician are still in force. He wishes to substitute new habits for old, in which the will to power remains the same but takes a more intelligent direction. This more intelligent direction will be one in which his energies are drafted more completely into the service of his higher powers, less into immediate subjective satisfaction, the process of "sublimation." It is also one in which he finds himself in accord with social ends—"socialization." And since he thus loses the need for concealment and duplicity, his energies are unified, division and conflict disappear, the man is "integrated." The priest has been inclined to express the result he aims at as "peace," reached through "reconciliation with God"; the analyst speaks of it as the "recovery of normal drive" reached through harmonization with society and with oneself.

Each has recognized that all unhappiness takes the form of inner conflict, and that cure must address itself to the sources of division. We find minor degrees of unhappiness in the milder forms of dividedness of mind—in the distracted man, the uncertain man, the indecisive man, the server of two masters, the man who cannot forget the lost good which he cannot recover. In its more serious forms it may be a struggle between higher and lower, a duty and an inclination, an inner and an outer requirement, with inability to give oneself fully to either. One can always regain poise by the resolute slaughter of all but one alternative. The struggle continues, and with it the distress, solely because one continues to believe that there is a "right" solution, arising from the nature of the problem. The priest indicates this solution in terms of the "will of God"; the psychiatrist in terms of human instincts and powers in specific social situations. The realigned habits need not be different in the two cases; but the priest takes into account the cosmic horizon of the individual life, which is frequently a factor in the problem.

4. *The Procedures Psychoanalyzed*

Let us now examine these three steps of procedure in the light of experience, that is to say, of the actual needs of the suffering person. First, to what extent is analysis equivalent to or superior to the confession of the church?

Confession is an acknowledgment of sin; analysis is a discovery of mistake or misfortune. Confession involves penitence; analysis brings escape from penitence. Confession remains morally difficult and does not emerge into an atmosphere of acceptance, nor even of scientific interest.

Now *causal* self-knowledge is a genuine part of self-knowledge; and often the relief it brings to excessive self-disapproval, a laming and unmanning self-disapproval, shows it a valuable aspect of truth. But if causal self-knowledge assumes to replace and dismiss moral self-knowledge, it has exceeded its province, and has gained one truth at the expense of another. It has falsified the moral history of the individual.

Analysis requires that the psychiatrist be the recipient of unreserved self-avowal. The psychiatrist assumes that his scientific attainments justify this demand on his part; he does not raise the question of his *personal fitness* to receive this confidence. But if he fails to recognize the pertinence of this question, he thereby displays his *unfitness* for his function. For here the moral issue cannot be merged in the scientific problem. It is neither desirable nor possible to confess all things to all men; it is least of all desirable to display one's sentiments before a gaze which is nothing-but-scientific, from which exposure *they can only emerge denatured, because pure science is indifferent to sentiment.*

Physicians have become the copious recipients of confidence of their patients in the tradition which was learned from Hippocrates, because the physician is chosen as a man, and not alone as a scientist.

Secrecy is, in fact, a normal part of life. Individuality is so much a private matter that even if we choose to lay bare all that we are, it is impossible to do so except to an attuned sympathy. There is such a thing as destructive secrecy: inability to let oneself go, whether in affection or hatred or anger, may become a preying inward fire.[1] Perception of this source of psychosis has carried our time to the opposite extreme. It is as if we had forgotten the fundamental fact of human intercourse that language is a voluntary act; which means that at every moment we—by necessity—control what we give and what we withhold. Selective utterance is the principle of normal communication. While there is destructive secrecy, there is also destructive confession, as when personal problems are exposed to public gaze or to a confidant unable to grasp their meaning. When one realizes that he has confessed to the wrong persons under the wrong circumstances, a new shame enters his life, and he avoids those to whom he has told too much. Thus maladroit confession lays the basis for a new disease. It is a recognition of this fact which has led some psychoanalysts to introduce an intermediate step of procedure, that of winning the love of the patient in order to secure his confi-

---

1. My tongue will tell the anger of my heart,
   Or else my heart, concealing it, will break;
   And rather than it shall, I will be free
   Even to the uttermost, as I please, in words.
   Taming of the Shrew, IV, ii, 78-81

dence, the stage of *"fixation."* The "patient then becomes
bound to the physician by the act of confession," and must
later be released, since the "fixation" is for a professional
purpose only. Upon which it is hardly necessary to remark
that unless attachment is sincere, it is a polite form of pros-
titution; and that confidences won by this device belong
to the destructive type of confession.

Of Explanation, the second step, we have already observed that to consider oneself as a phenomenon of cause
and effect is to see an important half of the truth. It remains true, as Dr. C. G. Jung puts the matter, that "to
understand the causes of evil does very little toward curing
it." We might add that there is a perceptible tendency the
other way, for the more successfully one sees oneself a
plaything of necessity, the less pressed he may feel himself
to change what, after all, is "human." It is well to know
what the usual practice is as well as what the standard is;
but if one must lower one's estimate of average fallible human nature in order to improve one's relative opinion of
oneself, the process of Explanation has surely omitted some
elements of just self-judgment, promoting content with
one's human fallibility.

It is in the third step, that of Re-education, that the resources of the psychiatrist reveal their chief weakness. To
say that the individual impulses require to be sublimated
or socialized or integrated is exact. But these are all formal
requirements. They tell you the direction in which nor-
mality lies, but they contain no substance on which effort
can take hold. "Sublimate your wishes, dear patient." "Yes,
but how does one begin to sublimate?" Plato himself was

far more specific: read the *Symposium,* and one is almost launched on the way of the transmutation of desire.

Or the direction may be, "Socialize thyself." But if one's trouble lies in the fact that his respect for social norms is abnormally weak, is a weak impulse to make itself strong on demand, or by tugging at its own bootstraps? As well say to the patient, "Be cured!" Or, to the disintegrated mind that it ought to be "integrated." But as John Dewey has well pointed out in *A Common Faith,* this is a job the disintegrated mind cannot do for itself. A distracted self cannot by applying distracted methods to its distractedness extract therefrom undistraction. Plurality operating on plurality does not produce unity.

In point of fact, the self-conscious psychiatrist realizes that he has here reached his crisis. The substantial thing which alone can bring about departure from the well-diagnosed malady is an adequate positive motive: a sound dominant passion will throw the lesser impulses into organic unity. The trouble with the the patient might be succinctly expressed as the absence of any such passion. The psychiatrist can accurately see the need, but as psychiatrist he has nothing wherewith to supply it. For it is not the business of psychiatry to say what life is about, nor what for any individual makes life worth living.

Here the wise and honest psychiatrist sees that he must get into another field. If he, as a man, has an adequate motive discovered elsewhere he may hand this on to his patient. If he has not, he is himself in the position of the patient and needs himself to be psychoanalyzed—a point which Dr. C. G. Jung has insisted on with such admirable insight. The whole issue of psychiatry, and of psychology on which it is founded, rests on objectives which lie beyond the mental states. No morbid "state" can be cured or altered by attacking it as a "state," *but only by attacking its object*. If the patient is worrying or afraid, he is worrying about something, afraid of something, hating something, desiring something; and to speak of "worry," "fear," and the like is to speak of half the fact, even when there is a subjective disposition to fear or to worry. A chronically shrinking or timorous reaction to the world hangs, for the patient, on a conception of the world; and correction of his ailment must address itself first of all to that view.

In brief, the problem of psychiatry reaches into the realm of meanings; and disturbed emotions must be set right by sounder objective valuations. If the world has a character which justifies hope and serenity, then fear and anxiety are to be met by indicating that character, as a necessary if not sufficient condition of any cure. If the world has not such a character, then the dominance of fear in the outlook is perfectly good common sense: with certain world-views men *ought to fear and worry*. And if one dreads the world he lives in and cannot change it, and cannot accept the silly advice to think of something near at hand and forget the frame of things, the psychiatrist instead of tampering with his emotions as such ought to advise suicide. There is no cure for mental diseases without consulting the total meaning of the world.

5. *Supplements of Psychiatry: The Logic of Confession*

Psychiatry cannot succeed on its own ground alone. It has brought to our age a new and brilliant demonstration of the truth on which Plato used to dwell, that sanity depends on organizing our desires under a dominant and stable affection. It has added to Plato that other truth on which the church has dwelt, that the way for that dominant passion must be prepared by confession, which faces and disposes of competing impulses. But its difficulty is that it cannot provide either the confession or the affection; each of these has its logic which prevents its use as an item of technique or a line on a prescription blank.

Confession is an act of opening one's life to the eye of a true judgment. If science is the true judge of life, then confession to one who represents science is possible. If science is a partial judge of life, if science in omitting the moral ingredient, omits an essential part of true judgment, then confession to the scientist must be by its own logic incomplete. Confession exists because at bottom men wish to know themselves as they are before a judgment of complete understanding and complete justice: they confess to those who most nearly reach that ideal, or who can most nearly represent it. The valid confessor must stand *in loco Dei,* where Deus means all morality as well as all science. The rankling center of mental disease is that one strives to cloak from himself what he cannot conceal from the universe: it is *that* pocket which must be lanced before integration can take place, and it requires an eye and hand more unsparing than that of condoning causality to do it.

It is true that the moral element of judgment may be so far censorious as to inhibit the beginnings of confession, and this may be the temperamental disqualification of the Protestant clergy as a class as hearers of confession. If the moral bones of the situation stand out gaunt and unrelieved as the doorkeepers of confession, they are out of place and out of proportion and therefore false. Their place is late, and their role one of quiet latency or suspense. The moral censor is apt to hasten to judgment on the basis of some well-boxed classification of good and evil before the facts are out; whereas there can be no justice until the nearby facts have taken their place in the wide swing of human experience and in the full uniqueness of the personal situation. It is this breadth of awareness and the patience belonging to it which the wise psychiatric practitioner brings to his "case." It is this, and not the substitution of causality for ethics, which the patient truly wants.

For in the end the moral issue has to be met, and no scheme which evades it can produce a cure or elicit a genuine confession. As Jung has so aptly put the matter: "The patient does not feel himself accepted unless the very worst of him is accepted too."[2] This word "accepted" is important; and here we see the benign mission of science. For science "accepts" good and evil alike, not as good and evil, but as parts of the great stream of the history of mankind. These things having come out of human nature are among the possibilities of human nature. Respect for such possibilities, and for the wide gamut of alternatives which the human will make for itself as it lays down its possible future, in respect for the groping area of life, is the fundamental morality both of the scientist and of the priest. The acceptance of fact must precede the rejection of evil within the fact.

2. C. G. Jung, *Modern Man in Search of a Soul*, p. 270.

The moral rejection must then follow, or there is no genuine cure: and this rejection must come from the patient's own conscience, not from any external rebuking agency. T. V. Smith has said that "a person with a conscience cannot be integrated because his conscience is always repudiating some part of his personality." The answer is, conscience is always repudiating some deed or other expression of the person—never any part of the personality—and repudiating it because it is a disintegrating factor, repudiating it in the interest of integration. For conscience is the awareness of the way toward integration, and of the obstacles thereto. We might therefore invert Professor Smith's dictum to read that *no one without a conscience has any hope of being integrated.* And the logic of confession requires it to gravitate toward a recipient who can represent the authority of conscience, whether that person be a physician, a priest, or a friend.

6. *Supplements of Psychiatry: The Logic of Affection*

We return to the point that psychiatry cannot reach a cure on its own ground alone, because that cure must lie in an affection which psychiatry cannot provide.

It has indeed tried to do so by inverting the ladder of Plato. Plato's re-education was a weaning of the soul away from personal loves and physical pleasures to a noble begetting within the eternal world of ideas. Psychoanalysis, on the contrary, finding the world of the patient's ideas awry, recalls the mind to personal and concrete attachments, dismissing concern for the eternal.

The instinct of psychoanalysis has a sound kernel, though

it has lost the clue to its element of validity. It is a part of the beneficence of nature that human love springs up in a sad world and gives to every creature at some time a taste of the ultimate good, within a local frame. What can thus glorify a forlorn career does tend to shed outward on the illimitable whole an aura of goodness, an aid to and a partial substitute for the elusive reaches of thought and faith. One may guess that sex-love is set into the world not as an apology for the miseries of existence nor as a back-fire against its endless perplexities as we face its total meaning, but as a symbol of the nature of things. What we read there becomes a part of our cosmic insight. Taken in this way, human love does work a cure on disordered spirits. Only, it cannot be set into a prescription!

Personal affection remains a matter of personal discovery: further, it is *derivative*. Persons as objects of love satisfy not because of what they are in isolation, but because of what they follow and believe in. We respect those who show respect beyond themselves; we love those who show love beyond themselves: they have their value as transmitters of an absolute good. If then the psychiatrist is to seek an affection which can unify a patient's life, he must discover somewhere in the universe a positive good which is objective, permanent, and total. The meaning of things descends from the whole to the part, and from the real to the less real.

The character of reality is indispensable in the object of affection. Life may be dignified by poetry: some form of art always stands between civilization and barbarism. But for the sick soul a prescription of the enjoyment of the beautiful as idea, even as Plato presents it, is futile. Hence when Jung says, "It is only the meaningful that sets us free" and then attributes that meaning to a fancy which he refers to as "the healing fiction,"[3] he is relying on a broken reed.

Now this is the difference between art and religion: that it is the real with which religion deals, while art deals with symbols of the real. It is in the end a man's religion which must finish what psychoanalysis begins. I am speaking here not of any special form of religion, but of religion in its stark minimal aspect, in which we may define it as a passion for rightness, and for the spread of rightness, conceived as a cosmic demand: God being that element of veritable demand which the soul of man immediately feels as springing from the heart of the real. It is only as this element of reality enters affection that it can do any healing work.

7. Conclusion: An Idea of God

It is not customary for psychology to distinguish, in its study of the emotions, degrees of reality. Is not a sentiment a sentiment whether its object is real or imaginary? Is not a fear a fear, with all its abdominal repercussions, even though it is a panic of delirium? If psychology should distinguish emotions as relatively real or unreal, it would be importing metaphysics into the laboratory, and its scientific status will be at once impaired.

It is precisely this which I propose to introduce into psychology in order to save its dignity as a significant human

3. *Modern Man in Search of a Soul,* p. 260.

exercise. Everyone knows that emotions do vary in respect to reality. The difference between sentiment and sentimentality has recorded itself in common speech, also the difference between the subjective and the out-living soul. A real emotion may indeed be excited by an imagined object, but only so long as it is believed real. When one consciously hugs the illusion for the sake of the subjective excitement, the emotion becomes unreal. It is this difference in emotional reality which makes the difference between self-flattery and a healing confession, between sex and love, between an experimental hypothesis and a working faith.

When we have made this requirement of reality in our emotional life, we have begun to realize how God can do work in the world without interfering with the procedures of science. For we say that in order to achieve its cure, psychiatry must organize the affections of the subject about an object which is real; no other object will do the work. But the real as an object of affection is what we mean by God. That is why religion must enter sooner or later into the work of psychiatry. It would be absurd to say that religion has been more successful in the cure of souls than has this branch of applied psychology. What we have to say is that *in so far as either has been successful it has consciously or unconsciously made use of the other*. And the time has come when the mutual supplementation may with advantage be recognized. Psychology in particular must recognize that feeling is essentially metaphysical, and that the whole emotional life of man is affected by that restlessness of which Augustine spoke until it has established its relations with the Most Real.

Perhaps this will amount to a step of religious advance also, preparing a new element in the conception of God. Fichte's definition of God as the moral order of the world has been felt too bleakly ethical, though not wholly untrue. May we not say that *God is the law of normal mental life?* We would mean by this that a life lived on the plan of getting along without God, without a sense of the cosmic demand, is already, whether it knows it or not, sick, off from normal, its values infected with the dry rot of mortality, intrinsically unhappy because unreal, driven subconsciously by a need which some day it is bound to recognize and define. This drive, which can be called psychologically the self-assertion of normal human nature, is in its true nature, the working of a law which is God. If this is the case, we may say of God that he is an unceasing activity, one which interferes in no way with scientific observation, but which is nevertheless indispensable to any complete psychological statement of what the life of man is.

CHAPTER III

SOCIOLOGY AND HUMANISM

---

1. *Society as a Moral Equivalent of God*

There is no possibility of mental balance in the human animal, so we concluded, unless there is some object outside him and beyond him which can serve as a focus for his affection. A ship gets stability by a heavy low-placed ballast; a purposive creature gets stability by an orientation ahead. We took that necessary object to be God. But the question is vigorously raised whether Society will not do as well or better.

It is agreed that psychology cannot define specifically what it is that men need; for psychology is and professes to be a science of partial facts. It proposes to deal with states of mind apart from the objects to which those states ordinarily refer. Thus, for such a state of mind as "fear" the concern of psychology is with the emotion, not with the miscellaneous array of situations which may excite it. It assumes that whether fear is stirred by earthquake, avalanche, explosion, sudden attack, the emotion itself has a recognizable mental cast which justifies at once the common name and the separate study. This relative independence of "state" from "stimulus" is a great advantage to laboratory investigation: to import earthquakes or cavalry charges into the laboratory would be cumbersome. When Doctor Walter Cannon wanted to study fear, he did it neatly by bringing a dog into the presence of a caged cat. In the end the dog, symbolizing fear-exciting-object-in-general, cancels out, and so for that matter does the cat, and only the "fear" remains, somewhat in the condition of the Cheshire cat's famous grin, though in this case even the feline quality is discounted. The point is that "fear" is a phenomenon with a pattern, and whether it be dog-caused-fear, noise-caused-fear, fire-caused-fear, or what not, that pattern has its own identity.

In most cases, this abstraction is wholly legitimate, so long as we remember that we are making it. But as we noted in our last lecture, there are certain important cases in which the attempt to detach the state of mind from its object falsifies the result, because there is *a unique object* from which the state of mind is inseparable. For example, there is a state of mind called "love," on the whole an important state of mind. Any psychology which shies away from it must be radically defective. But the notion of learning about love through clinical observation or through laboratory experiment begins to excite a sense of outrage. What "stimulus" are you planning to introduce, brother psychologist?

Or, consider that "dominating passion" which we found so essential to the healing of mental ailments, a state of mind not altogether different from love, how is such a state to be controlled either for experimental purposes or for prescriptions?

I enlarge on the nature of this dilemma because it is crucial for our time as well as for our own argument. It is seen clearly in a type of mental suffering or unhappiness, common during adolescence and the following years. It has no specific name—we say of such a sufferer simply that he "has not found himself." He is aware of having powers, he knows that they are not being used, but he does not know what they are. To be aware of unused powers is surely a state of mind, yet introspection is curiously helpless. What, pray, does a "native gift" feel like to its possessor before he has discovered what it is? Hardly anything more than a general uneasiness, impatience, refusal to become interested in the staples of education. But someday, more or less by accident, the sufferer encounters an object. He sees perhaps an artist at work, finds himself saying "I could do that," and power begins to run into an opened sluiceway. The psychologist can often aid this process of self-discovery by skilful "tests," an array of presented objects which may elicit symptomatic "reactions." But the results remain dubious just in so far as the objects lack reality. Ulysses S. Grant had latent and unknown military powers; it took the Civil War to bring them out. Unless the mental tester were prepared to introduce a Civil War into the laboratory as a "stimulus" he must have failed to detect Grant's point of genius. It requires the going world to discover the powers of a man, to himself or to anyone else.[1] Likewise, it requires the going world to cure

1. For a poignant example of this, done with characteristic quizzical humor, see Clarence Day's *Half Way Book* under the name Brown.

the sick soul. This is why the idea of God had to come into the reckoning.

But why go so far as God? Why not stop with Society? Agreed, a man must be cured by active relation with a real object, is not the human group such an object? It calls for loyalty, enthusiastic service, often for sacrifice. It has the great advantages of being tangible, verifiable, at hand, not an invisible entity which has to be grasped in thought. It includes and absorbs all the warmest human emotions; for family and occupation and all the images of memory and hope are set within the frame of what we call "Society." Assuming that there is a root of selfishness in all mental disorder—as there is—and assuming too that in all men there is a germ of disinterested care for mankind, why is not the rational line of cure that of "socializing" our too egoistic impulses? Instead of "God," read "Society."

Where in fact are the grand passions today? Are they in the God-worshippers, in the churches, in the monasteries? "The idealism of China is not in the churches: it is in the national movement," said a member of the Chinese National Christian Council in 1932. Kagawa made substantially the same remark about the idealism of Japan as he then saw it. Everywhere it is the vehement social movements which have succeeded in offering men a convincing object of devotion; and even those forms whose total direction is pernicious have rescued millions of individuals from introversion and the disease of meaninglessness. Every hot nationalism of our time, every fascism, Zionism, socialism, communism, acts as a cure for the intolerable subjectivity of the modern self-conscious individual. And if "religion" is the name for this rescue, it has less to do with God than with causes, leaders, and the impulses of great masses to move forward in concert.

For that matter, the major religions of today had in their origins a similar social quality. Their founders had a profound human concern. The dominating motive whether of Buddha or of Jesus was said to be *compassion* for the multitudes, and Buddha, we may remember, made no appeal to the conception of God. They themselves stood *in loco Dei* to the people around them, and cured them by arousing in them a similar passion for the weal of men.

The proposal, then, is that we find the necessary supplement of psychology in the social environment, and thus get along without God. Sociology becomes the fundamental science.

2. *Sociology as a Contemporary Science*

Sociology is an even younger science than psychology. It seems reasonable to suppose that psychology must do its work first, since societies have to be groups of individuals-with-minds. You cannot have a sociology of stars or atoms, unless with Professor Whitehead you are prepared to endow these units with mental characteristics.

But from another angle it appears that psychology cannot finish its work without sociology. No "mind" at the human level is possible without the experience which the human group affords. Individuals grow to mental maturity only by way of interaction and conversation. Language alone does much to make the man; and language means a social context. Apart from society, no psychology of human development could be traced. The two sciences therefore must help each other to completion: they form not so much a sequence as a coöperative pair.

It is this interdependence which gives sociology its claim to be a science on its own account, and not merely an application of psychology. It has an object of study, Society, which is not simply a collection of individual persons. There is some sense in the notion that Society is a real and verifiable fact, distinguishable from all the facts about the minds of its members. Naturally, unless "Society" *were* something, on its own account, it would be idle to bring it forward as a substitute for God. How are we expected to think of this something?

Undoubtedly societies have identifying qualities, like persons. Each one has an individuality which lasts while its members come and go, are born and perish; each one puts up a claim to an immortality its members do not have; it maintains that growing body we call "tradition" continually poured from past vessels into present vessels, with increasing wealth of meaning; it is wiser than any man, yet it both makes men and is made by them. It is the permanent container of the keep-worthy products of myriads of passing lives, and each of these lives gets a meaning because and in so far as it leaves within "Society" a deposit of created value, an idea coined into durable fact.

Are we then to think of Society as an over-individual self, having a conscious purpose and thought of its own, separate from those of its members? The difficulty with this notion is that such a being is nowhere findable nor addressable. If God is hard to locate, Society is not less so.

It neither speaks nor acts with such distinct agency that one can say, "This deed Society has done, and therefore neither you nor I nor any other man is responsible." There is no law, no work of art, no book, no thought which is ascribable to Society—no, not even the languages of mankind. Hence there are always those who maintain, in spite of the brave insistence of the new science that it is concerned with positive facts, that its central object is a figure of speech, a shorthand expression for the totality we human beings compose, and that to regard Society as a real being is but one superstition the more.

For present purposes, we intend to give sociology the benefit of the doubt. I suggest that we think of Society as a perennial vine whose sap circulates through successive generations of fruit-clusters. And since the "vine" in the wider sense includes its fruits, neither is the vine something without the grape, nor does any oncoming grape exist except as part of the vine it grows on. Society, in this sense is, as Aristotle said, "prior to the individual." And hence it is that individuality, as we know it, is modern. Individualism as a proud capacity to stand alone, to defy all tradition and all social opinion on the basis of one's private certitude—that is a late flowering of the race. In some philosophies of history, this self-separatism is equivalent to the Fall of Man,[2] the gradual loss of rapport with the central substance of life. In others, it is the highest point of advance. In any case, the great eras of group-thinking and group-feeling had to precede the emergence

2. As in the outlook of Gerald Heard, and to some extent of Arnold Toynbee.

of the modern individual, his will, his interests, his rights.

For the modern individual builds on self-consciousness; he is prepared to formulate his own goods and programs; he "knows himself" with a literal self-possession which in the Greek world was only a maxim and an aspiration. And this self-consciousness is no result of deliberate introspection: men see themselves in the mirror of their neighbors' eyes. They learn their characters by aid of the expletives developed in centuries of human speech. And even what their major passions mean becomes known to them only through those social patterns called customs in which their scheme of behavior is crystallized. Custom is the canalized flow of individual impulse into routes which permit the life of the same impulse in others. And I doubt whether the early establishment of custom had the extreme difficulty which Bagehot ascribes to it; for whenever a way of doing things is struck out which permits general practice, it tends to be hailed at once as *"the* way"; men see all things at first with an eye to their social use. Hence we have laws, institutions, common plays, labors, forays, honors, prestiges, condemnations—a substantial mesh of judgment out of which slowly human individuals lift themselves by acts of solitary self-perception and initiative. Society begets the individual by slow degrees.

Society therefore, whether or not it is a "person," is something quite real, so we shall assume.[3] And because it is something, it becomes the object of sentiments and pas-

3. I have undertaken to define what this type of reality is in *Man and the State,* chapter xxiv, under the head, "Will Circuits."

sions, the vital feelings of member individuals for their own rootage in the world. These feelings run deeper than consciousness, for they have to do with the continued origination of the personal mind; and the idea of "loyalty" to the Society is not so much a conscious expression of faith and gratitude to an outer benefactor as a recognition of organic continuity. Loyalty to my Society is loyalty to my own life. These are the facts which begin to concern religion.

Sociology deals with phenomenal facts in a causal world: it is not a science of values. But among its facts are the facts of human valuations. It has to consider the phenomena of common feeling, of the acceptance of rule and custom, of leadership and followership, of willing immersion of individuals in the Society and their adoption of its proclaimed goals and purposes. There is also for sociology a vast group of phenomenal facts called "religion," never separable from the system of social order; the "sanctity" of whatever is sacred, be it custom, property, law, kingship, or ritual, flows from the religious complex of ideas and feelings.

Now there is a pragmatic rule of thumb which has a direct application at this point: if two ideas have the same consequences, they are the same. If, then, "God" is a being who elevates and saves individual men through their devotion to the sources of their lives and culture, and if "Society" also is a being which elevates and saves through this same devotion, then God and Society must be two names for the same thing. God is Society in its persistent unity—inspiring, energizing, maturing the human individual, saving him from the futility of his intrinsic mortality through its own enduring care. This is the position of religious "Humanism."

3. Sociology and the Humanistic Interpretation of Religion

We cannot, of course, make sociology as a science responsible for religious Humanism. Sociology, in dealing with religion, simply reports what it finds; a group of unique facts of human behavior plus whatever it can recognize of the social functions of those facts. But since its scientific character prevents it from making excursions into the supernatural, it is limited by its method to such observing and explaining as can be verified within the social context. If religion were wholly occupied with a transcendent God, sociology could only report that the queer behavior of religious people, especially their ritual behavior, is apparently meaningless, one of the best examples of "conspicuous waste," and probably destined to disappear with enlightenment. Many sociologists, like Pareto, have in effect taken this point of view; and Freud has lent it support in his book *The Future of an Illusion*.

But the more sagacious sociologists have perceived important social values achieved through these mysterious performances and the ideas connected with them. Religion in early days has aided in the establishment of public order; it has proposed codes of law; it has supported the position of rulers; it has fertilized the arts; it has encouraged feeble humanity through the era of man's greatest weakness by offering him an alliance with the All-powerful. Whatever its secret may be, religion to a perceptive sociologist is certainly not negligible, not a "residue." Whatever God may be, the idea of God has released some kind of force into human life producing verifiable effects, coming to the aid of private effort, lifting it to a higher plane of power. "Inspiration," "enthusiasm," the influx of "mana," are genuine experiences, too useful to reject if, in a scientific age, they can be kept.

Ritual itself, the most obviously irrational aspect of human behavior, the first to be dropped by the sober positivist, is now being examined with a more hospitable scientific eye: perhaps it also has social uses. Lippert once suggested that the elaborate and costly rites of burial, requiring an extension of economic provision to a society of the dead even more numerous than that of the living, were something better than stupid waste, had an important function in developing foresight. Production was forced to create a margin beyond actual necessities, and saving became a human habit. Today we can see well beyond this somewhat strained utility. Ritual has to do with the emotional side of life; and emotion, as a response to value, is the most precious ingredient of life, the very stuff of which "welfare" is made. Ritual is employed in those passes of experience in which individual feeling is strained beyond its powers of expression, the crises of birth, puberty, marriage, death, initiations, celebrations, preparings for combat and for the great risks of wresting livelihood from nature. Feeling becomes adequate only when it is shared, in a certain unison achieved by established form. Ritual conserves the high moments of auspicious feeling, prevents the evanescent stuff of emotion from slipping away, puts all the best moments of the past at the disposal of the present. Thus ritual is the conservation of human dignity, and the recurrent renewal in experience of the depth of a civilization. It has ample justification on the purely human level.

Thus sociology, through its very method, facilitates the translation of religion to the human plane. It does indeed recognize the empirical fact—one of its most interesting data—that in past times it is belief not in society but in the supernatural which has done the useful social work. It is not incapable of giving an honorable place to the social achievements of well-devised illusions and myths. It can, for example, record objectively that Japanese soldiers fight well for the Sun-Goddess and her progeny, whether or not there be a Sun-Goddess. It may note further that, human imagination being what it is, most men do their best with some equivalent for the Sun-Goddess in mind. It depends on the sociologist's temperament whether like Pareto he imbibes the balm of mental superiority in looking down from above upon those human fallacies, superstitions, loyalties which do so much to lend the social machine its drive. But most scientists are more pained than pleased by this malign separation from their kind. They are infected by an inner honesty which doubts the necessity of the "vital lie" and holds to an unproved assumption that there is a *truth* to be had which will work as well as any fiction and be free from the poisons of superstition. Several such sociologists from Comte to Durkheim have actually proposed a restatement of religion on the basis of sociological truth.

But the actual humanization of religion has to be done by the religious spirit itself. It is religion, not sociology, which hungers for the accessible God, and finds in the newer sociological outlook materials to its hand. Thus we see Rabindranath Tagore, heir to a noble religion of Absolute Being, renouncing it in favor of a "Religion of Man" because he has seen that the work of religion in the world must be done by actual historical agents. In our own country religious humanism is spurred by a gathering sense of the unreality of the transcendental aspects of traditional religion. Many have been putting religion aside because the "acids of modernity" had for them, as for Walter Lippmann, made belief in an otherworldly God no longer tenable. Humanism came to them with an assurance that religion is not bound up with the belief in God, they may have the substance without clinging to the shadow—surely a gospel of emancipation. Religious humanism, with the aid of sociology, could put up a good claim to be the kernel of what religion had always meant and only now is able to express.

Since 1933, this movement has had a definite platform. We need not identify all of Humanism with this statement; but it is sufficiently characteristic to deserve our attention. We may take note of its first three articles:

1. Religious humanists regard the universe as self-existing and not created.
2. Humanism believes that man is a part of nature, and that he has emerged as the result of a continuous process.
3. Holding an organic view of life, humanists find that the traditional dualism of mind and body must be rejected.

Thus, in one-two-three order, are rejected the transcendent triad of God, freedom, immortality, the supposed staples of religion. And in their place, we find as the seventh article this:

7. Religion consists of those actions, purposes and experiences which are humanly significant. . . . It includes labor, art, science, philosophy, love, friendship, recreation. . . . The distinction between the sacred and the secular can no longer be maintained.

Perhaps we may summarize this view by saying that it is antidualism. There is to be no God-versus-the-world, no man-versus-nature, no soul-versus-body, no sacred-versus-secular; life is to be of a piece, and reconciled to its own conditions.

Yet it will not do to say that humanism has no dualism. It has its own "versus," for it believes in a higher-versus-a-lower in man. Without this scale or antithesis of value it could hardly present itself as a religion. It asserts that there is a battle within the all-comprehending unity of nature. The "merely" material, the "merely" economic, must be kept subordinate to the moral; the parts of life must be subject to the whole; social facts are not indiscriminately divine just because they are "social"; they must be dominated and ordered by a social ideal. Especially, there is such a thing as a complete personality. This has to be cultivated with reverence; and "reverence" is a specifically religious feeling which points away from the animal to the "spiritual" facets of our nature. It is this will to choose, and to fight for the choiceworthy, which turns humanism from a mere résumé of social science into a religious movement.

The advantages of humanism spring directly from the circumstances of its origin. It is no longer necessary to submit to the mutilation of being without religion in order to escape the strain of the supernatural upon one's mental honor. One looks at the field of right and wrong with a conscience unfettered by the commands of God; one is free to see the natural colors of behavior and the sound human basis for one's moral code. One is no longer tempted to defer to another life the rectification of evils which must be fought here and now. There is no "opiate" which can lull us into acquiescing in constructive social injustice; nor can we weakly throw our responsibilities upon an absentee Lord. Human life must find within itself the resources for its own correction and control. Man acquires the noble pride of self-dependence, and knows for the first time the awesome meaning of cosmic democracy in a world of the spirit from which kingship has vanished.

It is not a small matter that naturalness comes into religion and the smirking goodness of the Sunday façade becomes a thing of the past. Spiritual life becomes as direct and integral a part of oneself as the honor of honorable men. Nor is it wholly necessary that the word "God" should be laid aside, if one redefines that word to mean whatever works in human association to elicit and aid our aspirations, somewhat as John Dewey courageously did in his memorable tract, *A Common Faith*. For the period of transition, it would probably conduce to clearness to retain the old meaning of the term, whereby "God" is understood to be something beyond and other than "the world," and thus to accept the position that religious humanism is atheistic. This would be the preference of M. C. Otto of Wisconsin, who is still one with Dewey in feeling the vast importance of "natural piety" as a ballast in the orientation of man to his world. Nor would this be entirely an innovation. Early Buddhism was technically atheistic in this same sense, and for many an ancient and modern Stoic the same is true. If Humanism is sufficient as a religion, we ought henceforth to be able to get along without the word "God," since—if Humanism is valid—we are, after all, obliged to get along without God.

4. *The Working of Religious Humanism*

I suppose that for the first time in the history of civilized mankind, and perhaps in all human history, we have experimental evidence on a large scale to indicate how well it works socially to get along without God. There have always been atheists, but those who have professed their atheism have been exceptional individuals or groups. The atheisms of the Renaissance and of the Enlightenment were movements of the intelligentsia; that of the French Revolution was a lurid and transitory torch flame, so far as it reached the populace. But now in Russia we have had for twenty-five years the atheism of a great nation—not unanimous, but dominant. And in the socialist and nationalist movements elsewhere in the world, however their leaders truckle with religious organizations for political purposes, the secularist, atheist, humanist spirit of the youth-body which is their animating core is unmistakable. We shall, of course, know better after a hundred years, if Russia will remain atheist so long, how this régime works out. But meantime—and without committing the fallacy of identifying the Soviet system with religious humanism any more than it *is* identical—we can learn something of the way in which a great social enthusiasm makes a good substitute for traditional religion.

Of these experiments, the religious quality has been generally acknowledged. Fundamentally, they have given meaning to the lives of many individuals who have found our "individualism" running solitary and sterile. To be let alone to make out one's own happiness in one's own way— the great boast of liberty—begins to seem like the lonely inner life of a toper about whom no one cares. To be inserted even forcibly into a national or social effort is to have an emphatic tangible certificate of one's importance. Such incorporation into a living purpose integrates the man, elicits latent heroism, never lacks volunteers for the suicide squad, brings its fair quota of the human stuff well on to greatness. The vigorous social current tends to purify itself of its own original crudities and license, develops its own restraints and capacity for asceticism. In Mexico, Cardenas, simple, honest, and temperate, closes gambling places, sets himself against laxity. In Russia, marriage recovers a measure of stability, thrift some of its respect, science and art some of their independence; while the prevalent feeling that in spite of all mistakes, this land and this enterprise are "our own" makes possible an incredible popular effort of national defense. In view of these things, no one can deny that the active common cause served by a social group is able to tap the wells of moral idealism in plain human nature, which is a primary function of religion.

Reading the same facts from the standpoint of the group member, we see Society performing the essential functions of Deity, saving him from the egoism which is social death, inspiring him, making him a partaker in the immortal life of the whole, and withal protecting him as an enveloping Providence. As a protector, Society stands between the individual and the hardness of insensate Nature. From his cradle, his social environment is sensitive, living, responsive to his wants. For his sake it remembers, selects, accumulates the best of a long history, and in its "education" puts this at his disposal. Through its established routine of custom, it anticipates his needs and so answers his prayers before they are spoken. Like Nature it is in the main silent and unintrusive; but unlike Nature it is aware of him, and holds toward him a friendly purpose. When man found Nature capable of immense and unknowing cruelty, he took the edge from his terror by injecting a social element into Nature herself; he conceived a galaxy of Nature Gods. Society is the Nature Gods made real; through its laws and customs it achieves something of the impersonal regularity of Nature, while retaining its humane and conversible texture.

To this extent, we may say, Society does realize the meaning of religious experience, and shows substantial kinship with the traditional object of worship. To this extent, Hobbes was on the mark when he spoke of Society, organized under political headship, as "that mortal god, to which we owe under the immortal God, our peace and defense" (*Leviathan,* ch. xvii).

This is the positive side of the picture. There is another side, and this we shall now consider under the head of "dialectic." [4]

4. By dialectic we are meaning that effect of experience which is adverse to the assumptions on which we are going, so that we are obliged to revise them: I say to revise, not to cancel.

5. *The Dialectic of Humanism: The Finite God*

Experience as a teacher shows us a good many things we might not otherwise have thought of; but perhaps its chief excellence is that it reminds us of things which we might easily have thought of, and perhaps did subconsciously know very well. It is not otherwise with this "mortal god" of ours, whom we are experimentally setting up in a place of the immortal God. As long as the immortal God is there to fall back upon, we can endure the defects of the finite deity we call Society. But once we abolish God, we become acutely conscious that Society fails to measure up to the roll. The death of God leaves Society in the place of the Absolute; and like many another potentate who falls short of omniscience as well as omnipotence, we realize that his pretensions are tolerable only when he is humble and recognizes a law above him. Once his will becomes the definition of good and right, once the corporate selfishness of the state becomes the rule of virtue for the citizens, the moral individual knows that he is shut out from the free sky of his own convictions, and that a principle of evil has entered history in the guise of deity. Just in the moment in which Society is made an object of worship, just by that act man is warned that Society is something he cannot worship.

Like God, Society protects us and comes to our aid, so far as its knowledge and resources allow. But how far do they allow? Society has its cruelty, arising from its limitations, the more severe because it intends so well. It is never perfectly just because there is an appalling amount it never knows and can never find out. It is only partly responsive because it acts through men whose energy and patience give out. It knows how to deal with the usual cases of hardship in moderate numbers. When hardship becomes general, unusual, excessive, its hands fall helpless; it can only "do its best" like physicians fighting a pestilence. It is partly tolerant, but it feels safest with its own kind; it accepts strangers and its own inner strange folk with a reserve which delays adoption. In the end its best services command the price of conformity, and the nonconforming have to learn an aspect of repression which is in part born of fear. Society trusts itself but little on the waters of "dangerous thought"—a strange timidity for a God!

Just for the deepest wishes of the human heart Society has neither understanding nor sympathy. It provides for the group the current coin of culture; it brings to each doorstep the products of the thinkers and the artists; it offers amusements and the enjoyments of art: these are the daily bread for which its worshippers pray. The tame and common desires are ministered to; the wild are prudently trimmed away, and those who would cater to them are censored out of sight. This is as it must be in a world which must regulate itself by averages and probabilities. But there is another and fertile wildness, that of the *best* in man. That also is shut away. Society has not yet come in sight of the meaning of that best. Everyman somewhere finds the social pabulum limited, and is irked by the sense of an inner starving or warp which gets no relief. It is the total ciphering of Society at this point which begets many of those mental cases which then, by a weird psychiatric circle, are referred to Society for cure. But for all men, the

Providence of Society is superficial. Even language, its most perfect product, conveys only the coin of market and forum. It is just the unique individual who cannot speak, and remains somewhere the inner rebel and critic of the world.

Most men surrender in large part to the commonplaces of Society, accept a million petty compromises and ally themselves resignedly with the imperfect, because they discover none but this imperfect God. They may happily find somewhere a relieving version of Society, an individual friendship which gives breath to the suffocating regions of the solitary soul. A Society with personal love in it comes nearer God than a Society with nothing but social justice. But even so, this doubleness remains a defect in the deity; the halves of the soul are not brought together. It was this residual craving to which religion once brought its release. God was defined as he who knew "all men ignored in me." If then God becomes identical with "men" and their knowledge, this residual rebel called "the soul" must perish unsatisfied, and with it dies the most precious element of humanity, the growing edge of the self which is parent of the future.

It is one of the curious episodes of modern self-consciousness that Freud has well recognized and defined this function of religion, and then with a startling duplicity has poured scorn upon it. The strength of religious ideas, he says, is "due to the fact that they are the fulfillment of the most insistent wishes of man." What are these wishes? One gathers that they arise from the common failure of both society and nature to sympathize deeply enough with the subjective kernel of the individual; and because of this, the mature man wishes that the domestic canopy which in childhood protected and spoke to just these deeper levels of selfhood should be projected into the great world as its essential attribute. God is the image of a heavenly father "created by a continuation of the child's helplessness before his earthly father." Religion is thus diagnosed as an infantilism. Freud's shaft strikes not religion, but first of all the human self and then the universe in which that self lives. His judgment is that the "most insistent wishes of man" should, upon maturity, properly cease to exist. And why? Because the universe has no satisfaction for them. Freud should be taken on as a patron saint of Humanism. But as a psychiatrist, I suspect that the prescription, "Extirpate your 'most insistent wishes,'" will achieve few cures, and that the cost of taking such advice would be the loss of all the poetry, all the art, all the unborn beauty of the future race.

The result of this first step of dialectic is that Society in the role of the "mortal god," is not a satisfactory substitute for the God of individual souls. When the sun is out of sight, the moon makes a brave and apparently independent show as a source of light: but if the sun were abolished, where would the moonlight be?

6. *The Dialectic of Humanism: The Finite Fervor*

Like all religion, religious Humanism is concerned not alone with what men get from the universe, in terms of moral support, but also with what they give. Perhaps its chief way of ministering to individual morale is by way of cultivating the outgoing social motives which are in every man. Active religion includes the compassionate rendering of human aid by the individual; and no religion calls in vain upon the benevolent trait in human nature. For Confucianism, *jen* is the fundamental virtue. It has been translated as "humanity," "reciprocity," even "love"; literally, the character means the disposition to treat another as myself, a condensed Golden Rule. And Confucianism buzzes close to being a system of religious humanism.[5]

This social passion is a sound basis to build on. Sympathetic interest of man in his fellows is not alone universal, but provides its natural leaders. There are always a few in whom humaneness rises to the point of genius, who could say unaffectedly, "Write me as one who loves his fellow men." Secular Liberalism, itself a sort of religion of humanity, takes for granted the inherent goodness of human nature. Its creed is that to set men free, to develop their powers, educate them, assign them civil rights, is to release new springs of creative goodwill to the benefit of all.

Naturally, a feeling of this sort toward fellow men implies an objective judgment about their worth. No injunction to "love your neighbor" is obeyable unless the neighbor is in fact lovable. Christianity sustains its own injunction by the doctrine that each soul of man is valued by God, and therefore is, in reality, valuable. If we do not, in special cases, love our neighbor, the fault then is in ourselves and not in the nature of the neighbor. Humanism deprives itself in advance of this metaphysical support. It takes for granted that the spring of human kindness is

5. It escapes this by its persistent relation of the business of life to T'ien (Heaven) as appointer of individual life-tasks.

sufficiently copious and lasting to do its work without the benefit of divine authority; and that men are worth the benevolence thus poured out on them, solely because they are men, endowed with all the nobility of the species, and capable of responding in kind to the output of good-will. The humanist justification for faith in man is man's normal response to that sort of confidence, the impulse to be worthy of it. If one wants to make a good world there is no better way to begin—perhaps no other way—than by a firm, sagacious, and loving faith in human nature. Chiang Kai-shek's philosophy of Action transforms his army by dint of this one article: "Every man is capable of Action in the heroic sense, by the mere fact of being alive!"

Now this love of man, as a fact of psychology, has its peculiarities. It is not supposed to be selective, though all love is selective. It must make no concessions to impulsive dislike, even when my neighbor appears worthless, dumb, profligate, or criminal. It requires no personal acquaintance; it extends, as on principle, to all mankind near and far. Love for mankind might fairly be described as love of an abstraction, and as such to be rather a subjective sentiment than a positive force capable of doing work and carrying heavy burdens of coöperative enterprise. There are psychologists who say that there is in fact no such thing as a love of man-in-general, since all affection, as it descends from imaginary or romantically remote to actual objects, lights on kindred human types within racial or even tribal boundaries. The nation is the widest group anyone can effectively care for.

I doubt this psychology. I would rather say that man in

any racial guise is capable of arousing friendly devotion, on the basis of personal acquaintance. The difficulty which Humanism has to meet is not the diversity of human kind, but our limited capacity for acquaintance, direct or indirect. As an emotional fact, affection fades off from the center of intimacy to the vague periphery in which individuals lose themselves in an unknown mass. It is worth noting that the Teacher of Galilee never urged his disciples to love mankind. He had a good deal to say about one's neighbor; and he defined "neighbor" in complete independence of next-door-dwelling, also of race and tradition, but not in independence of human contact. Your neighbor, he taught, is the man you happen to encounter to whom you can be of service; he is not the man at the antipodes toward whom you entertain a wholly theoretical good will. As a psychological energy, the love of man is not capable of sustaining the unity of a great society, still less of mankind at large.

Nor can there be any cure for this situation on a psychological basis. The only remedy for the faltering, flickering, centripetal, ephemeral character of emotional benevolence is *a conviction regarding the nature of man*. Reason cannot substitute for feeling, but it can stabilize and universalize feeling. Humanism must therefore help out spontaneous benevolence, if it can, by a doctrine about the objective worth of human beings.

Now such a doctrine one does not find among the Fifteen Points of the Humanist Manifesto, unless we can read in it the staple theory of Liberalism about human equality. In the Manifesto, the end of man's life is said to be "the complete realization of human personality," the goal of humanism, "a free and universal society"; it will "endeavor to establish the conditions of a satisfactory life for all, not merely for the few." But the doctrine of equality is devoid of scientific standing. There is no measurable respect in which men are equal, nor can any data of sociology sustain the notion of human "brotherhood." For the purposes of lawmaking, the assumption of equality among the members of the community subject to that law is the most convenient, perhaps the only practicable, working hypothesis or postulate. This useful fiction is not available for a religion.

Sociology is totally helpless to give support to the kind of doctrine we need, that man has worth in himself. For sociology knows nothing about values, except by the way of human valuations. If somebody actually likes a man, the man may be defined as having value because of that liking; then if we cease liking him, his value vanishes: the sociological view of value refers back to that very psychological impulse whose fluctuations we are hoping to correct.

In my judgment there is only one way of escape from this circle. When we talk about the "intrinsic worth of man," we have to remember that man is a living being, an activity of intercourse with an environment, and that what we value in him, when we do value him, is not some static quality like his color or physiological set-up but something about the way he deals with his world. What a man "is" is inseparable from what he cares about and aims at. The worth of a cello-player in our eyes has something to do with the ensemble in which he plays, the music he can render, and his absorption in his art; he participates, let us say, in the worth of that system of things. To put the matter from the negative side, could we care for a man who cared for nothing in the wide world, and was incapable of caring for anything? Perhaps there is no such man. But the principle becomes clear that no man can have worth unless there is a worthful totality in which he devotedly participates, worth passes from the whole to the part. If the whole is worthless, no man can derive value from that connection. In a worthless world, no man has intrinsic value; and the purely factual world of science is worthless.

Obliteration of worth from the universe as a whole does not abolish human enthusiasm and love, as matters of fact. The saying is that all the world loves a lover. Let us expand this saying, it is *always* the lover whom we love; *we cannot love anyone except the lover!* The intrinsically valuable thing about man is his capacity for love—whatever form it takes, whether of persons, or beauty, or truth. The quality is infectious. Let but one person catch fire with love of something, then he can be loved by others, and they in turn for their love of him, until the whole world might be transformed by this one central flame. That is why, if you have a gift of human love, you can get the infection started, perhaps on the basis of a somewhat accidental interest, an infatuation, a footless enthusiasm. Perhaps the reality of the object of your emotion does not matter, since the emotion itself is what counts? No. Poor mankind, impoverished for the substance of worth, does in fact sustain itself largely by its enjoyment of enjoyers, and sets an inordinate value on these temperaments which spontaneously flow out in affirmations of value. But underneath lies the craving for *reality in appreciation*. If the precious essence is contaminated even slightly by effusiveness or professional amiability, it becomes hateful. The ultimate question cannot be evaded: Is the world worth our devotion? If you say, "No," the whole system of values is in for a slow collapse.

In sum, the love of man requires for its stability a truth about the world. If it is to do the heavy work of lifting humanity, there must be a trait of the universe which calls out effortless attachment and service; a trait which is there permanently and for all men. The word "God" has been used to signify this trait. But whether we use that word or not, the emotional basis of Humanism takes us beyond the human scene altogether, and requires us to concern ourselves with the nature of the cosmos.

The tragedy of human life is the law of entropy as applied to value, the running down of the capacity for love and joy. The deepest question about any man is, "How much can he care for anything?" If the answer is, "Very much," we bring out the word "genius," whose meaning depends on the rarity of its use. But genius loses its clue somewhere: X is astonished by his own triumph and lives in a fever of excess; Y is absorbed in his well-fitting topcoat, and accepts habitual instead of new admiration; Z is half-flustered by sidelong love affairs; M mingles the interest in ideas with the interest in cash-income from marketable words. Regretfully we bid farewell to our

prophets, one by one. Is it true, then, that all human mag-
nitude contains a factor of delusion?

Again, No. Fire can be kept if one becomes more rather
than less real; and this is possible in a world, and only in
a world, which has its own reservoir for the daily renewal
of devotion. Man is made for the infinite; with all that is
surveyable and enclosed, his fervors are finite, and burn
down to an ash. The infinite restores him to himself.

7. The Dialectic of Humanism: The Finite Frame

In substituting Society for God, Humanism plumes itself
on being realistic. Here is something that comes within
the scope of verifiable truth, almost of science. In this, it is
like many another self-styled realism, profoundly un-
realistic. It falls directly into its opposite, as a dialectical
experience ought to do.

For how can it be considered realistic to omit a good
half of the factual world with which men are dealing?

Humanism supposes that it is calling attention away
from the unknown margins of the world to the known
center, from speculation to the social hearth. But if God is
beyond-Society, Nature is not less so. Society, of course,
has its natural domain, but Nature stretches indefinitely
beyond all that Society uses. It is an untamed environment;
the infinitely vast and the infinitely minute elude us. We
explore them, we partly understand them, we never master
them. We do not forget that the God of tradition was the
God of men partly because he was the God of Nature; it
was through him that the unbounded was vicariously
brought under the domain of purpose. God's purposes

were not ours, but the point was that they were *purpose*, and therefore of a kind with our essence. Nature's refractory immensity and alienness were in principle subdued to the world of meaning. In surrendering God, Humanism turns Nature over to the unpurposing and the insensible, and the dread of a callous Nature resumes its full rationality. The man who does not fear the physical universe, on this showing, displays the "valor of ignorance."

We are, by a fine moral appeal, urged to forget what we cannot control. Whatever will happen to us out of the incalculable stellar spaces *will happen*—then forget it: our consciousness was given to us for the purpose of meeting dilemmas that emerge in our immediate foreground. The course of Nature, so far, has been on the whole propitious; the habits of our galaxy promise to hold for another million years. The principle of entropy is majestically deliberate and may have some sort of compensation: it is reasonable to expect good weather in our lifetime and that of our descendants. Forget the cosmic margin! There was a dervish who sold a sure cure for every disease; if his remedy failed your money would be returned. No one had ever come to claim his money back. All you had to do was to shake a pan of desert-sand for a half hour and during that time never once think of the word "hippopotamus." Forgetting by main will is a desperate performance. To forget what we do not know would be the death of scientific advance. It would be equally the death of human peace. If we could exclude the beyond-Society of the world from our attention, we could still not exclude the fact that we were excluding it. Refuse to think of the death of the race as we refuse to think of our own death, the one inevitable fact of our future: whoever advises this advises a violent unrealism, admitting thereby that realism would have an intolerable ingredient. There is something in the world he cannot face: forget it!

But the position of Humanism is even more paradoxical. It takes Society as something that can be defined apart from Nature. But what is Society if not man dealing with Nature in a corporate fashion? Is it not the common economic task which calls us together and outlines the sphere of our coöperation? Economy is not the whole nor the main business of Society; but there is no Society without it. Who is the farmer? Society pioneering with the soil, making the still miraculous transition from unusable to usable stuff. Who is the soldier? The permanent frontiersman against social and natural disorder. Who is the explorer? The social scout into unused regions. Who is the scientist? The frontiersman again who, afar off, sends knowledge where technique may sometimes follow. All these are social organs, making the world a part of "Society." The environment in which Society is now breathing is the wide universe. Nowhere can it draw a line in Nature and say, "Here I stop." Society dare forget nothing of that total in which its destiny is entangled.

Nor dare it forget that future in which its destiny is ever more deeply entangled with Nature. If Society, taken in its time-span, is a temporary passage in the vast night of evolution-and-dissolution, it is for us to know it, not to huddle away from it like huntsmen about their camp fire, pretending there is no stretch of black wilderness outside.

If a humanist asks whether it is not better to have lived than not to have lived, even if later one ceases to live; and whether during the time of living it is not better to give and enjoy kindness than to give and receive suffering, the answers are, "Yes, the better is better, so long as you are alive." But when you and the rest are nothing, there is then no better and no worse in your having lived; nor is the universe then better nor worse for your sojourn, if the universe also forgets. To suppose that there is anything better or worse in that future time is merely an illicit fancy that there is after all a cosmic memory, which is a partial reintroduction of a God into the world.

And the value which, at death, disappears into nothingness, tends for the self-conscious being to zero, even now. For he who must deliberately exclude cannot be single-minded; and he who cannot be single-minded cannot enjoy happiness. For happiness *is* single-mindedness in the appreciation of what is here and now, made possible by the fact that one has mentally faced the whole of experience and consents to what he has there seen as the truth.

Humanism would gain force for living by concentration; but concentration within a finite frame is only possible by the continued consent of the infinitude beyond it.

We have to thank the humanist movement for showing the defectiveness of any idea of God in separation from Society. It has taken seriously the fact of incarnation, whereby the life of God becomes a working element of human history. It has shown, too, *the perennial regenerators of religion* which are there in the social context of every life, all of them forms of love.

There is the concern of parents for children, which persists in hoping for a better-hold-on-reality than they themselves have had; their perpetual faith in a possibility we might call "diviner" if there were anything divine.

There is the inner meaning of the love between man and woman, not that religion is sex-love, but that sex-love at its best is religious, and knows itself to be an initiation into the deeper nature of what is beyond man.

And there is the up-reach of human life in patriotism and the service of social causes, in which morality is touched by a superhuman meaning.

But it fails to see that the authority of Society is derived. It commands allegiance because it obeys; it touches perfection only as it recognizes its own imperfection; it breathes only by way of the unlimited which it serves. Society can expect every man to do his duty, on one condition: that it speaks for a divine Will, which expects every man to do his duty. It is this being beyond Society which provides the staying power for a flagging conscience and a flagging love.

God is the law of a normal social life.

CHAPTER IV

ASTRONOMY, PHYSICS AND
WORLD-MEANING

---

1. *The Original God-Banishers Revisited*

It was physical science which first, at the opening of the modern era, determined to get on without God. It was the great emancipating deed of the seventeenth century to dismiss purpose, human or divine, as irrelevant to any hypotheses which physics or astronomy had to frame. Yet it is just to this field that we must now turn for the positive correction of an overconfident humanism, which takes too lightly the problems set for it by the cosmic frame of human life.

I mean by this in the first place simply that any picture of mankind which touches religion must take into account what the physical sciences have to say about the great universe as the scene of human life. We smile today at the disturbance which the innocent calculations of Copernicus stirred in the religious mind for a full century after 1543. What difference does it make to religion whether the sun revolves around the earth, or the earth around the sun? Not much, I agree; but what we call "man's place in Nature" is always relevant to religion. And so the questions, Out of what do we human beings come? How long is human life to last in the astronomical calendar? What comes after we vanish?—these questions belong to man's judgment of himself, and their changing answers affect his view of his total destiny. The bare facts and prognostics of descriptive astronomy do not wholly settle them; it would be foolish not to consult them.

I mean, in the second place, that physical science has something new to say about the place of *purpose* in the world-process. Not that the physical science of today is any more inclined than it was in 1700 to revert to purpose as a principle for its own explanations of events,[1] but that it sees that it can no longer *deny* purpose such a place, in our total contemplation of things. The logic of its own work compels it to recognize the possibility of purpose— and be it said that physical science is much better at logic than it was in the seventeenth century. It no longer takes for granted that expelling purpose from the equations of physical theory is tantamount to expelling it from the universe. What has happened is that physics (and let "physics" stand for astronomy also) recognizes its view

1. Biology since Darwin, it is true, is more or less tempted to fall back into the language of purpose because of the very device by which Darwin got rid of it. For when Darwin talked about "adaptation to the environment" and "fitness to survive," and rigged up his pretty mechanism of natural selection, he created a standing invitation to the physiologist to see the *usefulness* of an organic arrangement as the sufficient reason for its existence. Hence biology has acquired a shop-habit of substituting a means-to-end way of thinking for a cause-to-effect way of thinking. But with a rigorous scientific conscience it rejects any notion of an external purpose or plan, and insists that the "fortuitous variations" from which Nature selects the fittest (by killing off the less fit) arrive in the sober order of causal necessity. These lectures are incomplete without a separate chapter on the biological sciences. For the present I shall have to content myself with certain general references to the concept of fitness.

of the world as *partial*. It is partial, not because the two-hundred-inch reflector and its line of future successors will fail to discover the periphery of the cosmos, but because everywhere it deliberately omits from its view aspects of the truth which are certainly there. Physics used to think of itself as the most concrete of all the sciences, dealing with the veritable stuff of things as they are. It now sees that it is an *abstract* science, and for that reason cannot tell the whole truth.

For example, it limits the range of questions it proposes to answer within its own subject matter. Nothing is more the business of physics than "energy." And physics will undertake to say a good deal about how energy behaves, but about what it *is*—not a word. Advances in the analysis which aims at finding the ultimate units of physical being, having opened up a whole galaxy of subatomic *dramatis personae,* converge upon the electronic energy-unit as the typical world-stuff. If we ask a physicist what an electron is, or what a quantum is, or simply what energy is, he is likely to answer that his business is with the phenomena that can be explained by using these concepts in a set of differential equations, not with the inner nature of energy. Sometimes he passes the question on (with a vague hint of skepticism) to "the metaphysician"; or possibly he calls the logical positivist to his side, to assure the questioner that his question is strictly meaningless. But more probably, today, he recognizes that the question is both pertinent and significant—only, not in his field.

And if some philosopher proposes that physical energy has something in common, in its nature, with what we know as life, or are aware of in ourselves as mind, as has often been done in recent years,[2] the physicist will be tolerant of the hypothesis. Now and then a physicist will refer to the notion of Herbert Spencer that "the force by which things manifest themselves as existing" is of the same kind as "the force which manifests itself within us as consciousness," akin to Schopenhauer's older notion that physical causality is identical with what we know in ourselves as "will." And if some hardy seeker for first principles leaves the field of literal thought entirely and finds himself driven to symbolic and poetic expression, he will not be read out of court. The scientist may easily be restless or skeptical, but not dogmatically negative, toward such a statement as that from the newer *Logia,*

"Cleave the wood, and thou wilt find Me there,"

so reminiscent of the words of the *Chhandogya Upanishad:*

> That invisible particle (in the broken seed)
> That is the universal soul;
> That art thou, O Svetaketu.[3]

2. *What is it that Physical Science Omits?*

I believe it worth while to enlarge on this matter of the "abstract" character of physical science. For whatever is abstracted, or extracted, from a whole leaves something behind; and as we consider what physics deliberately

2. As by Lossky, Montague, Whitehead. One of the schools of Marxist philosophy in Moscow, teaching the "autodynamic" character of matter, might also be mentioned.
3. *Chhandogya,* VI, xii, 3.

omits from its province, the significance of the omission grows on us.

We were just mentioning that the *qualities* of the experienced world are omitted. To the seventeenth and later centuries it became clear that physics was destined to be a mathematical discipline and had nothing to do with color and sound as conscious qualities. Precise measurableness was taken to be a universal character of nature. This was never proved, it was assumed. It is still assumed and not proved. But the conviction grows into such a degree of firmness that any small differences from our calculations which events may show are immediately attributed to our own faults in calculating or observing, and not to any irregularity of the nature-process itself. (I believe that Heisenberg's so-called principle of indeterminacy constitutes no exception to this rule.) The disposition to take advantage of the incomplete predictability of some phenomena, especially the phenomena of life, as sign of the intervention of God has all but disappeared.

Indeed, it may be said that it is just the minute differences that offer the best footholds for scientific advance. For example, the chemistry of two generations ago presented the atomic weights of the elements as multiples of the weight of the hydrogen atom. The actual weights as determined by experiment came so near to whole-number multiples—carbon was 4, nitrogen 14, oxygen 16, etc.—that minute deviations in the third and fourth decimal places seemed a pedantic pretense of greater accuracy than actual technique could support. When Professor Richards announced his four-decimal atomic weights, there were audible murmurs: "Call it even!" Just these slight departures have become the footing for new chapters in chemistry. Again, the whole development of relativity-theory depends on a correction of Newton's simple formula for gravitation by a very small fraction. And the theory itself has as one of its tests a very small displacement of the apparent position of stars in the visual neighborhood of the sun, through the gravitative bending of their rays. Experimental support of the theory required a meticulous estimate of the extent of this displacement. The first test of this phase of the theory was to have taken place in 1914, on the occasion of a solar eclipse best visible in the Crimea. Professor Freundlich of Berlin was there with equipment to observe the eclipse. The outbreak in August of war between Germany and Russia placed him in internment, and the opportunity was lost. Soon after this disappointing event, Einstein found reason to make a small change in his first estimate of the small displacement. When the next eclipse was observed, the displacement was verified, and was found to be in close agreement with his *second calculation,* not with the first. The seeming misfortune of 1914 thus proved to be most fortunate for the reception of his theory; for the impression on the learned world would have been far different if Einstein's revision had taken place *after* his first estimate had been shown slightly wrong. So significant is the present meaning of almost indiscernible differences.

Thus the ideal notion once made notorious by Laplace of a world equation which should describe the motions of all particles in the universe through all time loses none

of its theoretical validity, though its attainment seems
yearly more remote. And if the physical network of all
history is thus in principle a matter of the most precise
determination, we are presented with a world-scheme
from which are absent not alone all the sense qualities of
sound, color, taste, smell, but as well all the feeling, passion, and meaning from which, for human experience,
physical events are inseparable. For man, no event is neutral; for physics no event is anything else.

This "bifurcation of nature" into quality and quantity
is no new thing; it was well known to Descartes, Locke,
Galileo. It was regarded as another way of reading the
difference between the subjective and the objective. The
world of quality was simply a mental affair, having nothing to do with the facts. Physics could fairly consider
itself to deal with the whole of the *real* world; the qualities
of things, especially the "tertiary" qualities of beauty,
worth, rightness, were subjective prejudices devoid of influence on the course of events. It is this easy reading of
things which the twentieth century destroys.

The plausibility of identifying the physical with the
real depended largely on the imaginability of the picture.
Everyone can imagine, or thinks he can imagine, an atom
flying through space. No one can imagine an electron,
nor picture in any model the nature of a quantum of
energy. Not only is physics a field of mathematics; it is a
field with which we can deal *only* by mathematics. It is
from physics itself that the query now arises, Can this un-
picturable world be, in truth, the real world? Gustav
Fechner once revolted against the "Night View" accord-

ing to which, since light is only there for consciousness, the whole physical history of the cosmos unrolls itself in darkness. Though the physical energy of light pours itself from all the suns over all the worlds, it is a light which illumines nothing unless there are "minds" to see it. Today, the protest is brought in the name of the integral Nature we know, not against a methodological theft which would deprive Nature of half of her being, but against the supposition that the physical half is anything more than an algebra of event. No one ever discovers a quality apart from a quantity, nor a quantity apart from a quality. Why then adopt the weird hypothesis that the quantitative is objective, the qualitative only subjective?

With this question, we seem to return to sanity. But if the real Nature is the Nature we perceive in its integrity, qualities and quantities together, then physics must present itself in the light of an abstraction from the whole. The revolt against the bifurcation which mistakes this abstraction for the real—a revolt strongly pushed by Dewey and Whitehead—is in part a revolt of observation against "abstract thought." It is in part, however, a moral revolt; for it seems increasingly incredible to common sense that the only things that have any importance—namely, feelings and qualities—are the things to be omitted from "reality." The real is unimportant; the important is unreal. This, we say, cannot be true.

3. *What, after all, are Space and Time?*

But this line of thought might well have failed to dislodge so well-established a conception of the world if it had not come to the same conclusion with another line of thought within physics. I refer to the new position assigned to space and time by relativity theory.

In the classical physics, space and time were entities in their own right, independent of the things and events located in them. That there were puzzles about their nature, everyone realized. They were evidently not "things," but rather non-things providing a room within which things could be. But they were also different from each other, two different kinds of nothing; and how nothing could have varieties it was hard to say. At any rate they were there, and in a logical sense were there *first,* before anything physical could either be or happen, since the world process had to unfold itself within the arena constituted by infinite space and endless time. For the same reason, space and time were eternal and unchanging, since everything in the nature of change presupposed their presence and stability as a background. If space itself were a moving thing, motions could obviously not be measured by reference to space; and if time "flowed" or "marched on" as it is sometimes reputed to do even today, then the flowing of events could not be measured with reference to time. In brief, it was thought, Nature *presupposes* space and time.

Now the twentieth century accustoms us to get on without these fixed regions of reference. It reminds us that we do not in fact either locate or measure events by reference to positions in space or time, for there are no markers in either. We locate events with reference to each other; we know intervals first and adopt positions afterward by purely conventional decisions; we know relations first, and terms as implied in relations. Further, as Minkowski observed, we know nothing of place except at a time, and nothing of time except at a place. Space and time are inseparable in experience, and as he proceeded to show, inseparable also in respect to measurement. What we have in hand is the concrete system of events. The abstract scheme of space-time against which we project this system is something we construct on the basis of the concrete data. Space and time thus lose their independence and their firstness for our thought; for our knowledge they are derived from events, and are not as Kant had said "ready in the mind" to receive the events.

It might still be true that what is secondary for our knowledge must be thought of as first in the order of reality. It still seems to us that, however slowly we arrive at the ideas, we recognize space and time as regions without which no events could take place, and in this sense as prior to events. But this reflection is countered by the awkward fact above mentioned—first clearly stated in Minkowski's memoir of 1908, and implied in the entire development of relativity theory—that space and time have no determinable or absolute quantities. The question, how far is point a from point b has no unambiguous answer, for we must first know whether we are to take them as at rest or in motion and in what time-interval the measuring process is carried out. Our answer will vary with the assumed position and motion of the observer.

We are driven, then, to accept space and time as abstractions from events. And the events themselves so far as physics is interested in them—i.e., in their centimeter-gram-second-measurabilities—are abstractions from the concrete experience of the observer. Physics begins with *his* observations, his sense-data, and if its calculations are right predicts future events which will be verified again in his sense-data. Physical science becomes an intricate system of theory enabling inferences to be made from one phase of experience to another. Then the real thing with which we have to do is not the intangible terms of the equations which embody this theory, but just experience in its immediate fulness of quality and meaning.

To some physicists, this means that physics is forced to return to the mentalism (commonly called idealism) of Berkeley and of Kant's Transcendental Aesthetic. Herbert Dingle carefully enquires how physical objects are "constructed" by us out of sense-stuff. Hermann Weyl asserts that the mental character of the world we find before us is the inescapable beginning of all rational thought about physics. Sir James Jeans is prone to exhibit the physical universe as a system of mathematical thought. Sir Arthur Eddington protests that there is one difference between a purely mathematical universe and an actual universe—one may be imaginary, the other real. But he proceeds to say that the only way we can necessarily distinguish the one from the other is that the actual universe has "the accent of consciousness." Hence the real remains even more emphatically the mental.

Whitehead and Dewey resist the drift toward mentalism, and insist that the return of the observer to the physicist's calculations does not require the absorption of the world into the observer's mind; it is still there in its full independence. It is premature to press this matter as if it were a foregone conclusion of contemporary physics. It is in my judgment inappropriate for metaphysics to take advantage of the embarrassments of a stage of physical enquiry which is so evidently in flux, and which involves so many makeshifts of terminology with which no one is very well satisfied. The late Professor Ehrenfest once said to me that the effort to teach mathematical physics in its present confusion had given him an insight into the Hegelian dialectic, "a succession of leaps from one lie to another by way of intermediate falsehoods." All that we need gather from the situation is the willingness of the most fundamental and characteristic branch of modern science to acknowledge the incompleteness of its own body of truth as a sufficient account of the "real world." When physics declares itself "abstract" in this sense, an epoch has taken place in human thinking.

4. *The Totalities of Pattern in Events: A Human Concern Which Physics Omits to Judge*

We have spoken as though all that is quantitative in the world comes within the domain of physics. This is not quite correct. Suppose, for example, a physicist were explaining to us some of the newer discoveries about the behavior of electrons, and we were to put the question, "How many electrons are there in the universe?" we might expect the answer (unless the physicist were Professor Eddington), "That does not concern me. I am simply interested in the laws they exhibit, not with their popu-

lation; their number may be finite, it may be infinite."
We might persist, "Of course, the total number could
hardly be known unless we had determined whether the
universe has a spatial limit, but the question of their
density or distribution could be settled without that
knowledge. Could you tell us the range of their concentration, let us say, from the densest portions of the sun to
the rarest regions of interstellar space; and how they are
arranged under each of those conditions?" Here our
speaker might reply, "Of course, the electron within an
atom would behave differently according to the degree of
propinquity of other atoms. We are much concerned to
examine these differences. But the actual facts of distribution of electrons or atoms belong rather to the history of
the universe than to physics."

Now the questions we have asked are quantitative:
How many physical units are there? How are they arranged? How much empty space is there, if any? And
why is there so much mass and no more, so many suns,
galaxies, dark clouds, or why so few? Physics gives attention to such questions, but it offers only fragmentary
answers. Its attention has been given to laws; it has taken
only a sidelong interest in *total quantities and "configurations,"* or patterns. Let the mythmakers play with the
constellations; science is unconcerned whether your fancy
sees a particular group of stars as a unit (knowing well it
is not a unit) nor whether you call the group a Great Bear
or a Great Dipper.

Nevertheless, physics has at least one strong vested
interest in pattern: it has a concern for *the repeatable* just

because it has a concern for law. For a law can be thrown into the form, "If A occurs, B follows; if temperature falls, water freezes." Such a formula makes no assertion that A ever happens, still less that it continues to happen; but it is evidently the business of physics to deal with what does happen, and the body of its theory is important just in proportion as it refers to conditions which occur or can be made to recur. It would not be too much to say that physics survives as a science only because it is successful in seeing the world of events as a scene of innumerable repetitions.

We may go a step farther. Some of these processes tend to reinstate their initial member and so to provide for their own recurrence. This gives us the special pattern we call a *rhythm*. All vibrations and swinging motions are of this sort, and movements of planets in their orbits. Rhythm often has the property of being compoundable, as small waves ride the backs of great waves, and the rhythm of day and night rides the great rhythm of the solar year. This property lends a factual foundation to the leap which human thought has often made from the part to the whole. May not the story of the universe itself be conceived as a vast rhythm, such as Herbert Spencer expressed in his law which was to include all laws—the law of alternate evolution and dissolution?

Physical science has hitherto been inclined to turn this question of total pattern over to the speculative thinkers, since it cannot yet survey the total universe at any one time, not to speak of a long period of time. And the speculative thinkers have tended to decide the question, not on scientific but on moral grounds. Some like Nietzsche have been attracted by the notion of Eternal Recurrence, *das ewige Wiederkehr;* the Stoics long ago had taught the periodic absorption of the stellar field into the great celestial fire, and the re-enactment of its play. But early Christianity set its face hard against any such cosmic cycle. It was asking a good deal to think that Plato and his school reassembled at long intervals to rethink their high thoughts and to be puzzled anew by the same ancient questions, having returned to the same original state of doubt. Somehow the winnings of thought ought to be *kept* by the world. The notion of repetition reduces the great work of Socrates to the level of the child's game; for the characteristic difference between work and play is that play, accomplishing nothing, is by nature repeatable. For Augustine, however, the deciding consideration was not that the idea of cycles made Plato repeat but that it made God repeat. Hindu speculation might conceive God as playing with his world, which was after all a source of partial illusion; but for Christianity the world is the scene of the labor and suffering of God in the tragic history of redemption. And whether or not Socrates might through innumerable ages repeat his struggle of thought from doubt to partial certainty, it was inconceivable that Christ should come and die again. His work, like every divine work, was "finished" and was so pronounced; it was done once for all time. To the Christian, therefore, the notion of a cosmic cycle was a crowning impiety.

Now science can have no interest in the ethical aspect of this debate. But it has certain comments to make on the factual situation which may help us in judging it.

First, it points out that all talk of repetition or rhythm

is a simplification: *no exact recurrences are known*. When science perceives and formulates a "law," it does so by singling out a facet of a process which in actuality may be endlessly complex. (This is another phase of the "abstraction" of science.) The earth returns each year to the same phase of its orbit, but not to the same point in space—if that phrase has any meaning—and never to precisely the same track with reference to the surrounding bodies. These surrounding bodies, each of which plays on the earth's motion with a different pulse, never repeat the pattern of their own positions. It might be imagined that after untold aeons some common multiple of the periods of these bodies would be realized, and a precise pattern of motion over great time announce itself. If the whole outer sidereal universe could be neglected, such a possibility is conceivable. But it is dashed by another consideration, with which contemporary astrophysics is now much occupied.

I refer to the fact that *some of the changes of the universe are unidirectional* in the sense that they cannot be reversed, and therefore prevent the recurrence of any processes into which they enter.

It has long been known that the available energy of the universe tends to run down, and that the state of universal equilibrium which this "increase of entropy" appears to forebode must be a state of universal death. Hence there has been much interest in the question whether there are compensating processes (short of the cosmic catastrophe on which Spencer relied to re-establish the original nebula) tending to restore what is lost. On this point we have no clear evidence. We can only say that the chart of the interplay of mass and energy is far more complex than when the second law of thermodynamics was first recognized.

But now a new question is raised: whether the entire sidereal system may be in process of expansion. Expansion and contraction are one-way processes, one of which points to a definite beginning, the other to a definite end. If the universe in all its parts were expanding at a known and constant arithmetical rate, it would be possible to calculate backward to a time when any finite segment of the universe must have been as small as you please. If on the other hand it were contracting, it would seem possible to predict a moment when it would vanish. The world of science adjusts itself with difficulty to either beginnings, or endings, having long been accustomed to the idea of endlessness in both directions. Professor A. A. Milne has proposed a way to reconcile the expanding universe with an infinite retrospect in time, by a regressive diminution in the unit of time-measure—an expedient which would raise a fair question whether something would not then happen to the corresponding measure of space. Fortunately, these are not questions which we need here resolve. It is sufficient to note that the scientific picture of world-change allows one-way processes a certain likelihood, and that where they are *present, cycles cannot occur*. This suggestion is confirmed by the third remark I have to offer.

This third remark comes not directly from physics, but from the mathematics of infinite collections. It plans to show that our existing system belongs to a class of patterns

which *cannot recur*. Roughly stated, it consists in showing
that the number of patterns which can be taken by a collection of electrons in space is in general far greater than
the number of moments in an infinite time series. The
possible patterns for even a small group of bodies moving
independently are too many to be run through in a continuous series of moments. This can be seen if one reflects
that a single body moving continuously in a line takes a
different position at each moment forever, whereas a
second body could be assumed to be in an infinite number
of different positions for each position of the first body, and
a third body in a similar infinitude of positions for each
pair-position of the first two, the number of possible patterns being multiplied by an infinite factor with each new
member of the group. Recurrences are possible therefore
only if the number of patterns assumable by the system of
bodies is restricted. If their mutual motions are tied together by such laws as gravitation, elasticity, etc., a given
system is limited in its array of possible patterns. If we
take four equal bodies and set them at the four corners of
a perfect square with zero velocity, then under gravity
and perfect elasticity the four are bound to move toward
the center of the square, click together at the same in-
stant and rebound precisely to the initial position, from
which an exact repetition takes place, and so on forever.
In general, symmetrical patterns will recur, and will be
at every moment symmetrical. In general, non-symmetrical
patterns will not recur and can never jump over from
non-symmetry into symmetry. There is an intermediate
class of patterns which are non-symmetrical but whose

stations correspond to fractional numbers or to recurrent decimals. These may follow a more complex recurrent pattern. But these symmetrical and proportional patterns, as we may call them, are artificially set up from the far more numerous class of collocations of which any ensemble of elements is capable. How seldom, for example, will a throw of dice even approximate a regular hexagon? Allow, then, that the stellar universe, so far as we know it, belongs to the class of irregular patterns. Just because it moves under laws, its pattern can never jump over into regularity, and it is *incapable of recurrence*.

Most children who speculate on the cosmos, and many of the grown children of past time who have thought of the subject, have preferred the symmetrical patterns as more beautiful. They failed to consider the fate of symmetrical beauty—a finite course of variety, and thus recurrence. It is only the irregular configurations that are endlessly fertile in new forms.

For the same reason, it is only an irregular world which can support a *history*. History is more than a series of happenings, it is a series with a meaning. And a series with a meaning is one in which meaning accumulates in the parts. In such a series there is no repetition. This is true even when parts of the series have a rhythm, as in the recurring night-and-day beat of human life; for the position of each recurring phase is different in relation to the whole movement. A second day cannot repeat a first day which had none to precede it. In history there are no exact precedents.

Thus, the present outlook of astrophysics favors the application to such stages of cosmic history as we can discern of the much-abused term "unique." We live in the presence of *das Einmalige,* that which occurs once only. It seems less probable than it did that other times and other worlds may be or have been the abodes of life, since the pattern of energies which here brought about the first living molecules may easily have been a unique pattern. And whether or not Henderson's argument for the biocentric character of the universe applies in full force only to this earth, it is still more probable that uniqueness may be restored to that much humiliated product of evolution, the human animal. Via the uniqueness of pattern-phases the astrophysics of the twentieth century does something to restore a geocentric picture which in the seventeenth century it destroyed.

5. *The Place for Purpose*

Irregular total patterns have the advantage of being always new, but there is in the fact of irregularity no guarantee that the novelties will be propitious. Chaos is irregular, and might conceivably have begotten more chaos through all time. If an irregular configuration moves out of shapelessness into describable form, that is because it was already "loaded" with that possibility. Irregularity by itself is irrational. From the standpoint of physics *any* pattern of the world is irrational in the sense that it has to be taken as pure fact. No physicist dreams of deducing the existing arrangement of stars or atoms from any rational principle. His highest hope is to deduce it from the next prior arrangements, and these from their predecessors, which leaves open the whole question why *this particular succession* of patterns exists, rather than some other succession, far better for us, or far worse. The total pattern is a *datum,* which is another name for an irrational.

Since physical law faithfully transmits the inherent irregularity of the world from moment to moment, we may say that for physics the whole story of the cosmos conveys a fixed burden of irrationality. It is a unique fact, out of an infinite number of equally possible facts, whose actuality instead of theirs is wholly devoid of meaning. Had we been able to intervene ten million years ago to the extent of altering the position of one hydrogen atom, the entire subsequent course of the world would have been different; and no one at that time would have been able to say that the universe as it was had any greater reason for existing than the universe after our alteration. Physics takes the pattern it finds and asks no questions; another pattern would have been equally acceptable, even though it might have involved—no men, ergo no physicists!

Once we are clear that physics renounces all interest and claim in the explanation of total pattern, and also that total pattern holds in it the whole issue of human existence or non-existence, we are prepared to ask whether this, for us, fateful enquiry must forever be left blank: *Why does this particular configuration exist?*

The answer may be suggested by the fact that the causal sequences with which physics deals reach no *goals.* That is why, for physics, cyclical and other reversible processes are just as satisfactory as the one-way processes. Where nothing is achieved, going backward undoes nothing; and men whose minds are thoroughly physicalized can work themselves into a state in which they fancy they are as willing to read time backward as forward. But purposive processes are irreversible because it is their nature to *reach goals,* and then to hold to what they have achieved.

If then the causal processes of the universe do something which it is not in their nature to do, achieve patterns which from our view are goals (such as the existence of life and human existence), and conserve these achievements; and if, as the preceding analysis shows, such attained patterns are involved in the original configuration of things—that "burden of irrationality" carried along by the physical process—then to interpret that whole "irrational" factor of the world-process as a purposive factor is a proposal to which physics can interpose no objection. Such a proposal would fill what is otherwise a vacuum of meaning.

But we should still hesitate to enter the vacant place unless there were positive grounds for doing so. Such grounds exist.

We may here recall the circumstance we have already alluded to, that science is itself a purposive activity and that its exclusion of purpose from its own business is a purposive exclusion. Outside of that special object, the exclusion ceases to be pertinent, and the grounds which led mankind to think of the universe in purposive terms resume their full force. The scientist cannot deny the nonphysical fact of his own purposes; and since purpose can never be extracted from causes, the existence of purpose in his own being has to be referred to an outer order of its own kind.

Beyond this is the fact of the interdependence of events and the nature of that interdependence. The extension of field-theory has brought into the picture of the universal interdependence involved in gravitation a more general interdependence of each event on all other events in the same light-cone. If any one event in that system is a "goal" all the conspiring events become related to it as the cells of an organism are related to each other. It is this which gives the universe the appearance of a society and forms the mainstay of Whitehead's "philosophy of organism." The togetherness of things is a significant togetherness.

Now certainly the whole of things is not a mere aggregate or collection of independent details—the new phase of physical science leads us to doubt the applicability of the word "independent" to any feature of nature, fully as much as does the philosophy of Josiah Royce. Quite literally the universe of electrons, which is at the same time a universe of infinite electronic fields, presents a minute (though no longer instantaneous) interdependence, justifying at once Whitehead's emphasis on togetherness and Francis Thomson's lines,

> All things by immortal power
>   Near or far
>   Hiddenly
> To each other linkèd are
> That thou canst not stir a flower
>   Without troubling of a star.

Yet I cannot follow this logic with Whitehead to the point of calling the whole an organism. There is more looseness among the parts of the world, more waste, wider flung oceans of emptiness, more *relative* independence than is compatible with organic unity. The inner rhythms and changes are not the proportioned movements of organic processes. What the universe seems to present is a true system of interdependent motions *within which* organic groupings take place and run their life course—the whole presenting the character of a *single environment* for the living fragments rather than being itself a total organism with no environment. What interests us is not that everything shall be living and of mental kind, but rather that the universe should offer itself as an arena for life and purpose, an arena whose very wildness, waste, vastness, unspanned gulfs of distance, offer incentives without limit to an ever-growing mentality. Seen in this way there is a purpose in the purposeless aspects of the world; the personal finds use for the impersonal, the living for the mechanical, the intense focuses of consciousness for the infinitely expansive unconsciousness of mass and energy-fields. If the world is definable as an environment for purpose, then by this definition it *has* a purpose, and is referred to a purposing being for its ultimate account.

To think of the universe as an organism is to think of it as the body of a life rather than as the object of a conscious subject. In my judgment, most of Nature is object and not organic body. It is something known, estimated, thought about, sought or shunned, named and adopted as "path" or "home" or "terra incognita" or "light-giver"

or "the tumbling main" or the "region of frozen glitter
and death"—all the furniture of meanings, adventures,
and the social welding of common dangers and efforts.
What happens to Nature when there are living beings in
it is its infinitely varied coloring according to its bearing
on our concerns. All those facts which were once mere way
stations or intersections of causal lines become charged
with goal-quality, positive or negative. The strength of
Whitehead's view is to show that this goal-quality pervad-
ing everything may *coexist with the causal scheme:* wherever there is consciousness, there purpose rides along with
the causal flood, and the movement of events becomes a
"creative advance." The weakness of his view is in his attempt to make everything at once goal and seeker, to
conceive all "actual entities" on the mental pattern, and
thus to ruin his noble picture of the ingressive goal-qualities which lure and guide the striving of the relatively few
foci of purpose.

His vision of the transformation of the physical by the
realization of qualities waiting to be born, as if Plato's
eternal ideas abandoned their impassivity and at the
touch of divine persuasion entered the world of change
and addressed themselves to our suffrages—this is Whitehead's poem and the valid message of his philosophy. The
universe is indeed a scene in which causal momenta,
repetitious and non-creative, form a mere core of the real
event. We have no full reality until conscious life sees
every object in terms of a glow of quality and *caring* turns
process into history. And the meaning of these conscious
centers and their striving is not seen until beyond their

factual goal-seeking, and through it, one perceives a non-material will, finding its own life in the solicitation of these myriads of beings toward the fulfillment of their possibilities.

What Whitehead has shown is that physical science cannot exclude such a vision. He does not show that physical science requires it, nor does he present his view as one which is proved by the evidence. He would persuade by presenting an "adequate" in place of an "inadequate" description of experience. He exhibits the bankruptcy of the traditional physics as a substitute for metaphysics; he presents his alternative with a challenge to all comers to do greater justice if they can to the infinitude of the world's qualitative wealth. He persuades by the amplitude of his hospitality to the abundance of universal possibility. He has made it impossible—one would like to believe for all time—to forget that goal-qualities and their responding purposes are an integral part of the concrete on-going of world-process.

6. *The Supplement to Astrophysics*

It is natural that a scientist should be content with an hypothesis in metaphysics. And an hypothesis such as Whitehead's which other scientists cannot reject, and which serves human life greatly by a firm comprisal of values with the facts of nature, has a strong descriptive appeal.

But it is still a description of something other than and distant from ourselves. The very sweep and majesty of its world-view lifts its object away from the simple immediacy of our living and our problems. Since it is cosmology and cosmography, it must remain conversant with the immensities and the infinitudes. This is one of its great merits. It recovers the nobility of the proper object of man's contemplation; in an age of minute specialization and of triviality masquerading as the height of man's achievement in analysis, it stands as a monumental rebuke to the seeming-wise. It "recovers altitude." In doing so, it recovers also the loneliness of altitude. It parts company with that illusory domesticity wherewith modern man deceived himself into thinking that his classifications and statistics were giving him a mastery of nature and of himself. It has shown the poverty of the cosiness of humanistic self-preoccupation. Nevertheless, without something of that domesticity, the universe remains hollow at heart; and what we only suspect as an hypothesis leaves the emptiness uncured.

I judge that this is the point on which Bruno seemed to his clerical associates to have missed the truth of things. Infinitude was Bruno's special point of piety, and also his point of heresy. To him, no one who thought God's work less than infinite thought adequately of God, to his colleagues no one who thought God's world shapeless and devoid of center as the infinite must be could think adequately of God. Bruno's world could have no domesticity, and a God dispersed everywhere as the "principle of connection among things" could not be found. It is indeed an incomplete God and an incomplete universe. What it requires, and what all cosmographical metaphysics requires, is a cure for the *illusion of vastness*.

This cure the mystics have always professed to have. To the mystic God is felt as an immediate presence. The voice of the mystic has little credence in the halls of high argument, for he declines to argue: he speaks simply of what he sees. He brings out no new categories, for he has no trust in any categories. He holds no brief for a more adequate description, for he denounces all description of the real as a misdescription. He rejects hypothesis, for he claims certitude and will be satisfied with nothing less than certitude. He makes a poor witness under cross-examination, and we do not bring him here for his testimony but we point out that we can have no confirmation of that of which we are in search—the presence of purpose in the whole of things—until the mystic's directness, immediacy, and assurance can be recovered in the common experience of men with the facts of nature. This step we are now in a position to take.

Let us recur to the position of those contemporary scientists who are willing to find themselves once more in the vein of Berkeley's "idealism," even to the point of sacrificing what they ought not to sacrifice, the objectivity of the physical entity. They are reliving the first insight of the modern revolution, that which discovers that the truly concrete thing is conscious experience, for it includes the object and in addition the enveloping awareness, "I think." Let us go with them to the simplest fragment of this conscious experience, the sense-datum, a single pulse of sound or of pain or of fragrance or of color. Surely this experience stands at the remotest pole from the astronomical reaches of the cosmos: it is local, punctual, immediate.

Now this sense-datum can be taken as a finality. It is the fact *par excellence,* the absolute kernel of what all "ideas" mean, and at the same time the absolute essence of agreeable-quality or disagreeable-quality, the pure stuff of value. Take it that way, and your humanity is firmly tethered to the earth. This is the hopeless way of beginning a philosophy, most plausible and most false. You have foredoomed your end by thus taking your beginning. The trouble is that the sense-datum is *not a finality.* No sense-datum is a simple, neutral, blank, opaque plaque of being. As a *"datum,"* it is something "given" and that means given to a receiving self by an outer activity; it is a surface of contact between a living mind and a living world. And because of this, with the quality is presented also *a moral alternative.* What! The sense-datum a moral problem? Just that. For there are two things in this one thing—the stuff, and *how I take it.* And there are two ways of taking it: as a subjective self-enjoyment—sinking myself in the sense-quality and becoming identical with it—or as a *summons to think.* If the sense-datum appears to me as a *phase of an object,* let us say the fragrance as the fragrance of a fruit, I have made a decision: I have resolved to live by thinking sense-data as signs of an object-world. This is the primitive moral choice. The life of the man and the life of science itself depend on rejecting the first alternative, and going in for the second; it is the rejection of solipsism, and therewith of solipsistic enjoyment; it is the beginning of conversation.

But if science recognizes the "ought" at the base of its own existence, it has asserted by implication that this "something beyond me" which gives the datum is a source of obligation. And only a living self can be such a source. This is not argued out by the incipient consciousness of the infant; its attitude is far more substantial and direct. It does the primary ethical deed of living outward rather than inward, as no proof could either require or reach, because it already perceives that which is not itself as a Thou, an Other, and accepts its destiny as a life of conversation with that Other. This is the immediate presence of purpose in the nucleus of the world, precisely there where science begins, and also the mystic.

It belongs to one of the conceptions of space dealt with in non-Euclidean geometry that a "straight" line indefinitely prolonged will rejoin itself at an assumed origin, constituting a vast circle. Let this be a symbol of the fortunes of the determined out-bound interest of physical astronomy, so trained away from all self-consciousness that the physicist habitually omits from his world-picture his own existence as a being of emotion and purpose. Just the sharpest physical analysis of today, just the utmost reach of penetration of the physical object, has brought the scientific thinker around *to himself,* first as an experiencer of sense-data, and then as a persistent duty-bound interpreter of these data, to set up a thought-world which shall be a public, a social world, a world for Other Mind. Without this element of duty, sense-experience would never become "science." Here, then, science—consciously or not—responds to a cosmic demand. There is, as the breath of life for science itself, an *ever-acting law of normal thinking,* a non-interfering activity, in the requirement for a truth which shall be "objective" truth. And here again, the experiment of getting on without God has led to a new perception of his presence.

At the same time, whoever thus perceives the infinite universe as an edifice of truth to which our momentary feeling and thinking are instantly responding has been cured of the illusion of vastness, for he has touched, as directly as sensation itself, the garment of the living God.

EPILOGUE

The modern mind would have far less trouble with the idea of God if it were not persuaded that to be real is to act, and that to act is to have discoverable effects. The word, God, must stand for something real: it must therefore stand for a being who acts, or whose very nature is activity. God cannot be an eternal Idea, a synonym for Perfection, everlastingly alluring but internally abstract. On the other hand, if God is a doer of deeds, a worker in history, a factor in the affairs of men, he threatens the hard-won clearway of science. This constitutes the dilemma with which a scientifically sophisticated age like our own is confronted.

Now religion has long recognized that there are paradoxes in the nature of God; that God is both eternal, always the same, and yet active, and that his action is at once "omnipotent" and silent. If science is concerned with such overt action as can enter the scene of cause-and-effect, God is not one of the factors in any such scene. This would make him a competitor, and a finite force. To describe God in terms of superlatives in such an area, as "the Greatest Power," would be to mistake his mode of action altogether. God conquers Thor, the mighty drinker, not by being a greater drinker, but by being the sea which Thor's goblet cannot drain. God is irresistible because he is non-competing. As Lao Tze said, Tao acts *by nonassertion.*

One way of expressing this noncompetitive relation is to say that God acts through a noncausal dimension. An imperfect analogy is that of the light which projects a motion picture onto a screen. The activity of the figures and objects on the screen is causal. The light does not interfere with that action; it does not contend with any of the powers there active. It sustains the whole panorama of events. If it ceases, there are no causes and no agents at all on the screen. They all depend on it, and it is not one of them.

In some such way we may consider the constant activity which we experience in sensation, the raw stuff of conscious content and also of physical experience. A sensation can be regarded as a blank-counter, a neutral essence, a static plaque of being, simply *there,* and answering no questions as to its provenance. It is "datum" and there's an end of it. Such a position is a dogma, not an experience. For experience, sensation is *received;* it is a datum in the literal sense of something-given; it is there as a result of an activity from without. That activity is not causal, for causality plies between sense-objects. This primary and universal and incessant presentation of the stuff of being is an activity of God.

The sequence of sensations is a part of the causal pattern, so far as we are receivers of it. But what that sequence is, is laid down in the pattern of the whole. This total pattern does not determine itself. If any part of it is a deed, the whole of it is a deed, a single and consistent act of decision, and therefore of purpose.

This being the literal element in God's action, the second mode of his action becomes possible, that of serving as a real object for the emotional structure of the human mind, and therefore as a source of stability and health in individual and social life. Our earlier discussions showed this need; it was only in our last discussion that we found how it could be fulfilled. What the psychological and social arts of our time require for their success is a simple fact about the nature of the world we live in, the presence there of a total and divine purpose. Given this fact, then the argument which we have called the "dialectic" becomes an epitome of human experience, personal and also historical. It is the silent and perpetual conversation of God with man. It is the endless restlessness of the soul unable to satisfy itself with the goods of the first look; a constant rediscovery of the perishability of the finite objects of affection. But since that rediscovery is from ever new phases of sensitivity and exploration, the recovery of reality is no mere repetition of ancient lessons of experience; it is the creation of new qualities and the arrival of new truth. And in that joint work of the finite and the infinite, an element of adventure may enter also into the life of God.

INDEX